kids' crafternoon
beading

kids' craftemoon
beading

25 projects for a crafty afternoon

edited by Kathreen Ricketson

hardie grant books
MELBOURNE • LONDON

Contents

introduction **6**

tools and materials **6**

basic techniques **13**

safety **17**

pep your look **18**

nifty necklaces **46**

spruce your space **64**

giving is good **102**

Introduction

Kids' Craftemoon Beading brings together a range of attractive and fun projects. Some are easy and some require a bit more skill and patience, but all of them incorporate beads in interesting and exciting ways. You will learn techniques to make different styles of jewellery, as well as beaded ornaments, window hangings, bags and more. You will be sewing, gluing and threading your way to becoming a beading genius!

Tools and Materials

The nature of beading means you will need to be quite organised. You should keep your beads separated out into little containers, use a good desk lamp and sit in a comfy chair. When you go into a beading shop it is easy to become overwhelmed with all the shelves of different sorts of beads – and some of them can be really expensive too. You might wonder what all those little bitsy findings are for? Plus there are lots of different tools and other things… Do not fret, this book will break it down for you, simplifying what you really need to get started and will showing what you can achieve with only a few basic tools and beads purchased for just a few dollars. Also – all the projects in this book can be completed with just a few simple tools.

PLIERS

A set of jewellery pliers will come in handy for many of the projects in this book. You can get these from craft shops or hardware stores.
- Wire cutters – for clipping wire and cord
- Flat-nosed pliers – for flattening and squashing and angling wire and beads
- Round-nosed pliers – for forming smooth shapes.

SCISSORS

Scissors are needed for cutting fabric, cord, paper, thread, fabric and elastic. Tweezers are needed to help with knotting, gripping cord and picking up beads.

GLUES

Glue will be needed to attach beads to fabric and findings. You can find jewellery cement glue at beading and craft shops. Also, regular PVA craft glue and a hot glue gun are essential items.

Hot glue gun and glue sticks. Nothing quite beats the instant satisfaction or the permanent fixing ability of a hot glue gun. While a hot glue gun is an extremely useful craft tool, it can cause burns so careful usage is essential. As a general rule, a small amount goes a long way and you should avoid your hands coming into direct contact with the glue. When using a glue gun, put some pressure on the surface after you have applied the glue for a few seconds, this helps to make it stick to the object.

PVA craft glue. PVA is a non-toxic multi-purpose glue. It can be used on all sorts of surfaces including wood, paper, fabric, felt and beads. It goes on white but then dries clear and can be painted.

Multi-purpose jewellery glue. Multi-purpose quick-grip glues are fast bonding and strong; however, they can be toxic and should be kept away from small children and used in a well-ventilated space. Ask at your bead or craft shop for a recommendation or try these brands:
- E6000 is an industrial-strength cement-glue that is commonly used in jewellery making, but it requires a 24-hour curing time
- a non-toxic alternative is Pritt multi-purpose glue
- note that Super glue is an adults-only glue, as it requires precision and can be dangerous if not used properly.

STORAGE CONTAINERS
Keeping your beads, findings, wire, string and other jewellery bits organised is essential in beading. You can use a fishing tackle box or small plastic containers with snap-on lids – these can be found easily and cheaply at a hardware store or craft shop.

BEADING MAT
While making your beading projects, it is essential to use a felt mat so that your beads don't roll right off the table and onto the floor. You can get a felt beading mat from a beading shop, or simply use a large piece of regular craft felt. When finished, roll it up and keep it with the rest of your beading supplies.

BEADING NEEDLES
When sewing beads onto fabric or doing any loom beading, you will need to use a needle and thread. A regular sewing needle is just fine, but make sure that once threaded it will fit through the hole of your bead. For loom weaving, a longer needle is quite useful as you can fit many beads on your needle at the same time.

Specialty beading needles are available at craft and beading shops, these are usually longer and finer than regular sewing needles. For tiny seed beads you will need a slender, narrow eyed beading needle (size 10–15).

HAND SEWING KIT

Some of the projects in this book require a little bit of hand sewing. You can purchase a sewing kit already made up at a craft or sewing store, but it's easy to make up your own kit.

Sewing kit supplies

Keep all these sewing supplies in a small plastic container, a sewing basket or even a clear glass jar:

- Small scissors
- Pins stuck into a small square of felt and folded in half
- Hand sewing needles in a couple of sizes and your beading needles
- Sewing and jewellery thread
- Thimble
- Pencil.

IRON

You will use an iron with your fuse beads. Remember to press and rub gently and use an ironing board or lay out a towel onto your table.

JEWELLERY FINDINGS

Jewellery findings are the small pieces other than beads and chain that are used to make jewellery, for example: fasteners, clips, crimps and clasps as well as jewellery blanks, like rings and earring hoops plus a whole heap more. These are available in a huge range of sizes, colours and types of metal. As a beginner you might want to stick with one type that you like best, then you can gradually build up your collection.

Jump rings. These are used to join two pieces together – like a bead onto a chain. Jump rings are small circles of wire that are not fully enclosed. Use two pairs of pliers to open the ring, attach it to your bead or chain then close it again with your pliers. Choose a medium size for the projects in this book.

Ring and brooch backs. These are simple backs with a blank flat front where you can glue or sew your design.

Earring findings. These come in a variety of styles and designs suitable for pierced or un-pierced ears. Earring wires have a split loop at the bottom end, like a jump ring. Open the split loop sideways, rather than apart, using your long flat-nosed pliers, and attach your earring design, then close the loop with your pliers.

Clasps and fastenings. With so many different clasps, toggles and fastenings to connect to your chain, wire or corded necklaces and bracelets, it is very easy to get confused. They can be quite simple or ornate, and provide different ways of attaching. Depending upon the type of stringing material you are using, clasps can be attached with the help of a jump ring, a knot, or a crimp fastening.

Crimps. These are small round or tubular shaped metal beads that are used to secure a fastening or a bead in place where a knot isn't appropriate, they are also used to space beads where you don't want them bunched tightly against each other. String the crimps onto your wire, position them where needed, then use flat-nosed pliers to press them into place.

CORDS AND WIRE

When stringing or chaining beads and pendants and garlands, there are many different materials you can use: from ribbon, cotton string and leather cord to wire, elastic and chain. All of these are available at regular craft stores.

Craft wire or coloured enamelled wire. This wire is pretty easy to find and inexpensive too. It comes in all sorts of bright colours and is very pliable and easy to work with. When buying wire, remember that the higher the gauge number the thinner the wire will be: 26 gauge (0.41mm) is very fine wire and great for delicate beading projects with small beads, it's super bendy and pliable; 20 gauge (0.81 mm) to 24 gauge (0.51 mm) are good medium weight wires that hold their shape really well and can thread onto most medium sized beads. 16 gauge (1.25 mm) to 18 gauge (1.02 mm) are really good for more structural projects and for larger beads.

Chain. This comes in all sorts of shapes, sizes and colours. You can buy it in bulk or in pre-cut sizes with a clasp already attached. Use it to make necklaces, bracelets or hanging ornaments and attach beads onto it with the use of jump rings. You can even sew it onto fabric!

Elastic. This is very convenient for basic beading and comes in many thicknesses and shapes: Fine beading elastic comes in different colours and thicknesses and is very strong; it is useful for a whole heap of different beading projects. Craft elastic is a bigger, corded elastic that is great for chunkier projects.

Fibre, leather and fabric threads and cords. These come in different thicknesses and lots of different colours and varieties:
- Waxed cotton is a good basic cord to have for stringing and knotting.
- Leather, suede or faux leather cords are smooth and mostly waterproof, use them mostly for larger beads, pendants or charms, you will need a crimp clasp to fasten.
- Hemp is a very durable and tough string; it is great for knotting projects.
- Ribbon and fabric are so versatile; use sheer organza, velvet, grosgrain or twill ribbons instead of cords to string or sew your beads onto, also try braiding ribbon and fabric to make textural, colourful bands.

BEADS

Beads are the be-all of this book. There are so many different varieties, shapes, colours and materials. For the projects in this book you will need a few different types of beads and remember these tips:

- Add to your bead collection a little at a time.
- Beads can be threaded, glued or sewn, so be sure to check the project specifics before going shopping.

Wooden beads. These are great to use as a base for collage, fabric wrapping or painting. Or use them as they are for a natural look.

Acrylic and plastic beads. These are cheap and cheerful and come in all shapes, colours and sizes.

Seed beads. These are tiny glass doughnut-shaped beads; they come in a few different sizes and can be bought cheaply in bulk. These are often used for bead weaving and sewing projects and for friendship knotted bracelets. They also come in different finishes – like pearl or metallic, for example.

Pony beads. These are larger than seed beads and are either glass or plastic. Pony beads are usually bright and colourful and fairly cheap and versatile for all sorts of projects.

Bugle beads. These are thin tubular shaped glass beads approximately 1–2 mm wide. They are perfect for sewing to fabric and are also useful as a spacer bead on a threading project.

Glass and metal beads, crystal and semi-precious beads These up-market beads are wonderful to use for special projects. They tend to be more expensive, so use them sparingly and collect a few at a time.

Organic and 'found' beads. Examples include driftwood, natural shell, nuts and even seeds. Found beads are fun to play with. Drill or poke a hole into them then thread, or wrap wire around them, to form a pendant. You can also find shells with natural holes already in them.

Flat-back beads are jewel-like beads. These beads can be real crystal but are more commonly synthetic. They have flat backs that make them useful for gluing onto surfaces such as ring findings or even fabric.

Buttons. Use buttons just as you would other beads. Buttons are great to incorporate into your beading projects – for stringing, gluing or stitching. You can get sparkly ones, natural ones, and plastic, painted, metal or glass buttons. Collect vintage buttons on your trips to second-hand stores.

OTHER MATERIALS

As well as all the wonderful and varied beads and the few essential beading tools, there are a few other craft supplies that you can find at craft stores that will add to the fun of your beading experimentation. They include fuse beads, shrink plastic sheets, polymer modelling clay and mixed media.

Fuse beads. These small plastic fusible tubular beads (Hama and Perler are common brands) can be used for stringing projects and are also great to use for bead weaving, but they are more often used in fusing projects to make small motif designs. Place them in your chosen design onto a bead board, cover with baking paper and press gently with a hot iron. They fuse together and you can make charms, pendants or ornaments from them.

How to use fuse beads

1. Place your beads on to the pegboard as per your design. Use tweezers or a toothpick to help you pick up and place the beads more easily.
2. Take your bead board to your ironing board then cover the beads with baking paper.
3. You must follow the safety advice when using your iron. Set your iron to a medium heat and keeping the iron level, gently iron the beads in a circular motion for about ten seconds. Rub the iron gently over your design until the beads begin to fuse.
4. When you think the beads have all fused but the holes in the beads are still visible, lift up the corner of the baking paper carefully and check if any beads come away; if they do, replace the paper and iron for a few more seconds. Leave the beaded fabric to cool on the board for a few seconds before removing.
5. Turn your design over, cover again with the baking paper and repeat the ironing process on the reverse side to strengthen it. To make sure the design lays flat, place it under a heavy book for a few minutes while still warm.

Shrink plastic sheets. Shrink plastic (Shrinky dinks is a common brand) come as clear, frosted or coloured sheets (or in special kits), and can be drawn or printed on and cut out. Be sure to choose the correct product for your project. Place your designs on a baking tray and heat in the oven for two minutes while they shrink to about a third of their size and nine times their thickness.

How to use shrink plastic sheets

1. Draw, trace, stamp, colour or print your design onto your shrink plastic sheets. If you want to trace a design use the frosted see-through sheets, and if you want to photocopy or print a design with your ink-jet printer, make sure you get the correct product for that.
2. Cut out your design using scissors. Remember that your design will shrink by a third. Punch any holes in your design at this point with a hole-punch, as you won't be able to put them in later.
3. Pre-heat your oven to 160° C, you could also use a toaster oven but do not use a microwave oven.

4. Place your shrink plastic shapes onto a baking sheet with the coloured side facing up. Put it into the pre-heated oven and keep watch – it only needs a couple of minutes.

5. Turn on your oven light so you can watch as your shrink plastic design shrinks and curls and then eventually lies flat again. This process will not take longer than 3 minutes. Remove from the oven with a heatproof glove and place a book or other heavy object on top while it cools for a minute, to help it stay flat. If you need to pick up the designs while still hot, use a pair of tweezers or your heatproof gloves. Use your shrink plastic designs in your project.

Polymer modelling clay. Polymer modelling clay (Fimo and Sculpy are common brands) is used to make all sorts of small sculptural objects including beads and trinkets. It comes in lots of different of colours, which can be mixed together to create cool patterns. Once the shape is made it is then baked in an oven for about 30 minutes at 110°C to harden it. It can be painted after cooling.

How to use polymer modelling clay

1. Create your design as per your project instructions. Making your own beads from modelling clay is a really fun project, where you can experiment with colour by twisting, bending and cutting the clay colours together to create all sorts of marbled designs. You can also work just with white clay, as it can be painted with acrylic paints after baking. Before baking be sure to poke beading holes through the clay with a BBQ skewer as you won't be able to do this after it has hardened.

2. Preheat your oven to 110°C. Place your clay designs on a baking tray in the oven for 30 minutes. Use heatproof gloves to remove the tray from the oven and leave to cool before touching them. Be sure to read the instructions on the packet as baking times and temperatures may differ from brand to brand.

MIXED MEDIA
Combine fabric, material and paints for a 'mixed media' approach to your beading projects.

Fabric scraps. Some projects in this book require fabric scraps for embellishing and collage. Tiny scraps are perfect – ones left over from other projects. Collect bright, happy cotton fabrics and ribbon for use in these projects.

Ribbon. Ribbons are used in several projects in this book. Grosgrain ribbon is a very strong woven ribbon available in most fabric and craft stores. Other craft ribbons or even strips of fabric can be used as well. Read the project specifics before going shopping.

Leather or faux leather off-cuts. Off-cuts of leather or fake leather material can be handy. You will use a few scraps for a couple of the projects in this book. You might be able to pick up leather at a second-hand clothing store. Luckily, leather can be painted to get different looks. If you can't find leather or faux leather pieces, try the hardware store for vinyl off-cuts to use as a leather substitute in these projects.

Felt. Felt craft sheets can be found easily and cheaply at craft stores and come in a huge range of colours. Felt can be used in beading projects and a felt mat is a useful item to prevent your beads rolling around.

Paints. Acrylic paints can be found in general craft and discount stores. Start with the basics – black, white, blue, yellow and red – and mix your own colours. You will also need some paintbrushes, plastic trays and an old shirt or apron to protect your clothing.

Basic Techniques

The techniques used in this book are basic and fun to master. Ask for help if you need it. Some projects will provide alternatives to using the trickier techniques.

ATTACHING CRIMPS, CLASPS AND JUMP RINGS

Crimp beads are small soft-metal beads that are squashed onto the beading wire or cord. They are used as spacers in between beads to separate and hold beads in place, or used to create loops and to attach clasps to the end of a project. Often you will need to thread your wire or thread through a crimp twice so make sure your crimp has a big enough hole for the wire you are using.

Making a loop at the end of your beading piece

1. Take your crimp bead, and slip it onto the end of the beading wire. Add a clasp or jump ring.
2. Loop the wire back through the crimp bead, leaving a small amount of extra wire as a tail.
3. Press the crimp hard and firm with your flat-nosed pliers; flatten it well. Turn it over to press it a second time, so it doesn't slide, if necessary.
4. Trim the tail of the wire and hide it under the first one or two beads that you string on.

Adding a crimp closure for leather and cotton cord

1. Use flat-nosed pliers to press a crimp closure to each end of your cord – with the ring facing outward.
2. Attach one half of a clasp to each end of the crimp closures, you may need a jump ring as a go-between, it depends on the type of clasp you have.

Adding a regular clasp onto string or wire

After you have strung a length of beads for a necklace or bracelet, you can add a clasp.

1. Check the length of your strung beads, then take off the last bead strung, thread on a crimp tube, replace the bead you just removed, thread on another crimp tube, then one half of your clasp.
2. String the end of your cord back through the first crimp tube, the bead, and the second crimp tube. Make sure the crimps are snug against the beads and squash them with your flat-nosed pliers. Repeat this process for the other end of the cord, using the other half of your clasp, and trim the ends of the cord.

Opening and securing jump rings

1. To open your jump rings, use two pairs of pliers – one in each hand. Open the jump ring by slightly twisting it. Move the open section of the jump ring side to side, creating a gap in which to insert your chain, charm or jewellery finding. If you just try to pull the jump ring apart, it won't snap back together correctly.
2. Insert your jewellery finding, chain or charm and twist the jump ring closed again using both pliers. To really secure the jump ring, position it so the join is at the top of the pliers then carefully squeeze the jump ring to slightly reshape it into an oval shape.

WIREWORK

Twisted wire can have a very useful and pretty effect, and it is used in a few projects in this book. You can twist wire around stones, gems and shells to create beautiful pendants, or you can twist two lengths of wire together to create a very strong base or frame for a project. If you are using very thick or strong wire you will need to use your pliers to wrap and twist and bend the wire. However, if using craft wire you may be able to use your hands.

Twisting wire

1. It is better to start with a wire that is too long than too short. It can always be trimmed to remove the excess length when you are finished. Use a good stiff wire so it will hold its shape.
2. Fold the piece of wire in half and make a loop at the folded end by twisting the wire a couple of times.
3. Nail a large nail into a piece of wood half way and place the loop over this nail, or you could hang the loop onto a door handle – something to hold it as you twist. With your hands (or pliers if the wire is too strong to twist your hands), twist the wires around each other evenly, swapping them equally back and forth, so they remain the same length at all times. Try to keep an even tension as you wrap, so that one section is not tighter or looser than the rest.
4. Once you have finished twisting the wire you can shape it and use it for your project.

Wrapping wire

1. Find the centre of your piece of wire, and bend the wire in half at that point.
2. Place your shell or stone inside the bend of the wire

and pull the wire securely around it, where the two wires meet twist them together tightly a couple of times with your hands or your pliers.

3. Bend the twisted section of wire up, then run one wire diagonally across the front of the stone and the other wire across the back to meet up again. Twist the wires again a couple of times.

4. Take one wire and wrap it across the front then around one side, ending at the back. Take the other wire across the back and twist the two wires together tightly. End with one wire pointing straight up and the other pointing down and out of the way.

5. Bend the wire that is pointing up downward, to create a loop (use your pliers here) and wrap the tail around the shaft of the wire to neaten and strengthen it.

6. Take the other piece of wire and wrap it around the entire stone including the wire loop, about 3–4 times. Clip off any excess wire and you are ready to hang your pebble on a cord or chain.

STITCHING AND KNOTTING

Adding buttons and beads to your projects is a very attractive way of embellishing and adding your own personal design touch.

Sewing on a button or a bead

1. Using a pencil, mark where the beads or buttons will go. Thread a small needle with about 60 cm of sewing thread, and double it over so you have about 30 cm of doubled thread, and knot the end. Make sure your needle and thread will fit though the bead hole.

2. Pull the needle through from the back of your material at the marked spot and up through one hole of the bead or button. Put your needle back in through the other hole of the button or directly next to the bead and back through your material. Pull the thread firmly. For added strength for buttons and larger beads repeat this process three times through each hole, but for small beads once is enough.

3. Repeat this process for all the beads you wish to add. Finish by pushing the thread through to the back of the material then, before pulling the thread tight, threading your needle through the loop of thread and pulling tight to form a knot.

Running stitch. This is the simplest and most commonly used hand stitch. Pass the needle in and out of the fabric, keeping the length and the space of the stitches even. When sewing beads, as you bring your needle up through the fabric, place one or more beads onto your needle before pushing the needle back through into the fabric.

Square knot. The square knot, also known as a reef knot, is one of the most basic and useful knots you can learn. It is the most commonly used knot in macramé and is worked with two strands of cord folded in half to form four strands. The two middle strands are inactive, they don't do anything; the outer strands are the working strands, the ones you knot with.

To make a square knot you first tie a left-handed overhand knot followed by a right-handed overhand knot or the other way around. Make sure to alternate between a left-handed and right-handed overhand knot otherwise your bracelet will form a twist.

1. Bring knotting cord A across both filler cords and under knotting cord D (see diagram 1).
2. Bring knotting cord D under filler cords B and C (see diagram 2).
3. Bring knotting cord D up between filler cord B and knotting cord A. Pull on A and D to tighten them (see diagram 3).
4. Bring knotting cord A over the two filler cords B and C and under knotting cord D (see diagram 4).
5. Bring knotting cord D under the two filler cords B and C.
6. Bring knotting cord D up and out through the loop between A and C (see diagram 5).
7. Pull the knot tight.

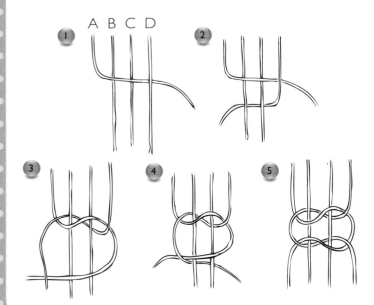

Making pompoms

You can make pompoms with just your fingers, or you could use a special pompom maker if you have one. You will need colourful wool or acrylic yarn and some scissors.

1. Place your index and middle fingers together and hold the end of the yarn with your thumb, wrap the yarn around your fingers with your other hand, but don't wrap too tight or you might cut off your circulation. Wrap the yarn around about 70 times, then cut it off.
2. Cut a 30 cm piece of yarn and push one end in between your two fingers that are wrapped with the yarn and the other end in between the tips of these two fingers. Wrap the yarn all the way around the middle of the bundle and tie the ends together in single knot.
3. Slip the yarn bundle off your fingers and tighten the knot, then tie a double knot to secure it.
4. Holding the pompom with the yarn strings you just tied, take your scissors and cut through all the loops on both ends of your yarn bundle. Fluff it up a bit it will look a bit of a mess at this point.
5. Neaten up your pompom by trimming it all around with your scissors so it becomes a round ball of fluffy yarn.

SAFETY

With all tools and equipment there is some safety required in using them. Some of the tools and equipment mentioned here are hot and very sharp and need careful and considerate usage.

ELECTRIC TOOLS SAFETY TIPS

An iron and a hot glue gun can cause burn injuries if you are not careful. Be sure to keep these tools away from younger people and keep the cord away from tripping feet. When you are finished unplug them and put away after they have cooled down.

- Use hot electrical and sharp tools on a high, stable surface such as a bench or table. Don't use them on the floor.
- Unplug any electrical tools immediately after use. Remember to allow time for them to cool down after they are turned off.

GLUE SAFETY ADVICE

- Wear protective clothing and protect your work surface when working with glue, be careful to hold the glue over the table surface to avoid dripping it onto your skin or clothing.
- Only use it on the table, never leave it on the floor or in reach of younger people. Always put the lid back on after use and put it away properly.
- Hot glue and jewellery cement glue can give off toxic fumes, so make sure you work in a well-ventilated space.

SAFETY TIPS FOR USING SHARP IMPLEMENTS

When using scissors, pliers, needles, craft knives and other sharp implements:

- Always put your tools away when they are not in use.
- Do not walk around carrying sharp tools or wave tools around while talking.
- Watch where you are working; keep your fingers out of the way of sharp tools.

pep your look

Satisfy your inner fashionista by making accessories to mix and match with your outfits, with cute earrings, badges and rings. Groove your thing with Bird of Paradise earrings, express yourself with a leather badge or by wearing a bold Lego ring! Whatever your style, you can shake it up a bit with these fun items. Personalise each design or make them as they are – it's up to you!

The projects in this section range from super easy to a bit trickier. None of them are very difficult, although some designs might take a bit more patience than others. Some projects require a hot glue gun or a needle and thread. If you aren't sure about anything read the techniques section first and ask for help if you need it. Don't fuss about perfection, the aim is to be creative, make something cool and enjoy the process. So grab a snack, pop on your favourite tunes and get crafting!

Bird of Paradise Earrings

Lego Jewels

Woven Zigzag Band

Storm Jewel Set

Pizzazz Hair Ribbon

DIY Badge

Bird of Paradise Earrings

These exotic bird earrings are made with fuse beads. If you haven't used fuse beads before don't worry, they are super-easy and fun to use, and available in most craft stores. Once you master this simple technique for making motifs and attaching jewellery accessories – nothing can stop you from developing your own awesome designs.

project by: nicole vaughan
suitable for: beginners
should take: less than 1 hour

SHOPPING LIST

- 2 earring findings
- 2 jump rings, each 0.5 mm
- Fuse beads and pegboard

CRAFTY NEEDS

- 2 pairs of flat-nosed pliers
- An iron (use a small craft iron if you have one)
- Baking paper

GET READY

- Gather your tools and materials and clear some space on a sturdy worktable. As you are working with beads and other fiddly bits, you will need a clean space to work on and perhaps a felt mat or hand towel to stop your beads rolling everywhere. Make sure you have a comfy chair and some good lighting too.
- This project requires the use of an iron; take care when using an iron, as it can cause burns. Read the safe handling of craft tools section on page (17) and be sure to put everything away when you are done.
- Fuse beads are joined together with an iron. Find more detailed information on using fuse beads on page 11. Be sure to read the instructions on the packet before using. You will also be using some jewellery findings, which can be found at bead or craft shops, and you can find basic jewellery techniques on pages 13–14.

HOW TO MAKE

1. Use the diagram provided on page 23 as a guide to placing your fuse beads on the pegboard. Cover your beads with baking paper and heat for a few seconds with your iron. Wait for your piece to cool before removing it from the pegboard, flip it over, re-cover it with the baking paper and heat set the other side with your iron.

2. Make another design, this time in reverse to create a pair for your earring set. Once you have made your first one, copy the reverse side to create a pair of mirror-image bird motifs.

3. Take two sets of pliers and gently twist the jump ring open (don't pull it apart). Attach the jump ring to your bird through the hole in the topmost bead, then slide an earring finding on to your jump ring. Use the pliers again to close the jump ring and you're done! Repeat for the other earring.

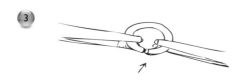

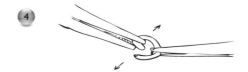

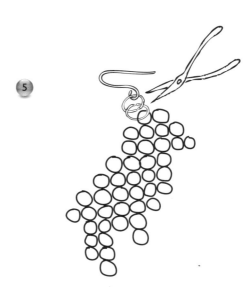

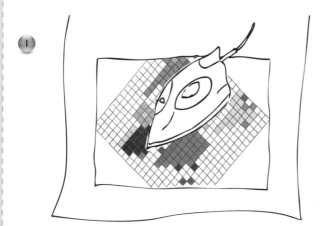

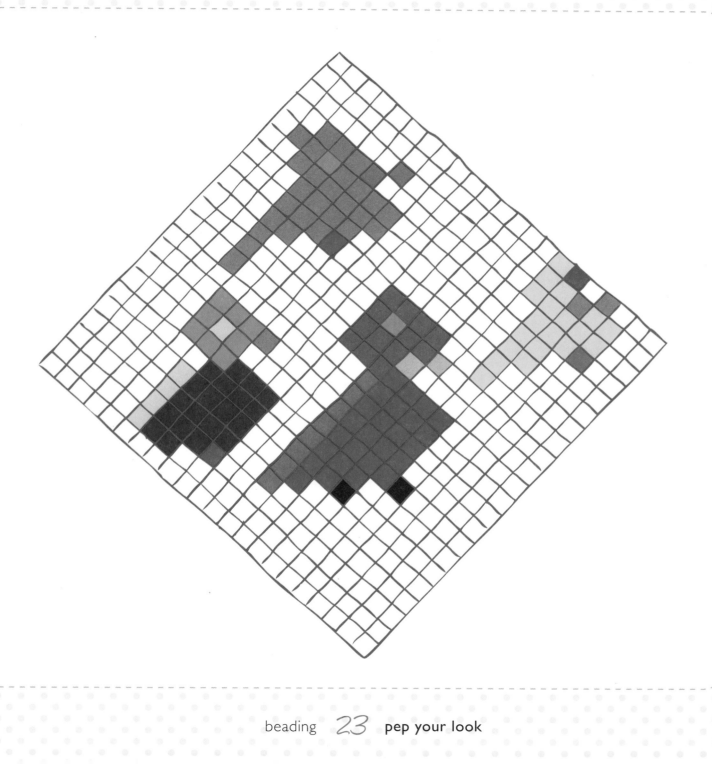

Lego Jewels

These crazily playful jewels are made from regular old Lego! You surely have some lying around somewhere. Once you start making these addictive designs you will be whipping them up for all your friends. It's a simple technique that involves Lego and glue – what could be easier, or more fun?

project by: nicole vaughan
suitable for: beginners
should take: less than 1 hour

SHOPPING LIST
- Blank ring findings and brooch backs
- Small Lego pieces or figurines

CRAFTY NEEDS
- All-purpose jewellery glue

GET READY
- Gather your tools and materials and clear some space on a sturdy worktable. As you are working with beads and other fiddly bits, you will need to work on a clean space. For working with glue you should wear protective clothing and cover your workspace with newspaper. Make sure you have a comfy chair and some good lighting too.

- You will be using a strong, all-purpose cement glue for this project. Take care when using cement glue, as it can give off toxic fumes. You must work in a well-ventilated space. Read the safe handling of craft tools section on page 17 and be sure to put everything away when you are done.
- You will be using brooch and ring findings, which can be found at bead or craft shops. You can find a description of basic jewellery techniques on pages 13–14. If you don't happen to have any Lego on hand, you can use this technique for converting other small plastic toys to jewellery. You could paint mini dinosaurs and plastic beetles – in silver or gold, for example – for some extra bling!

HOW TO MAKE

1. Option one is super quick. Grab a small square Lego piece in your favourite colour and your ring or brooch finding (see diagram 1), get your all-purpose cement glue (or your hot glue if using) and put a dab of glue onto the ring or brooch finding pad. Place the Lego piece onto the pad and gently press down (see diagram 2). Set aside to dry.

2. Option two involves getting a bit fancier with your Lego creations. Stack a few smaller pieces of Lego to create a mini sculpture that you can wear as a ring. To create a permanent Lego sculpture, dab a little bit of glue onto the peg of the Lego pieces before clipping them together (see diagram 3). Also try using mini Lego figurines in your designs.

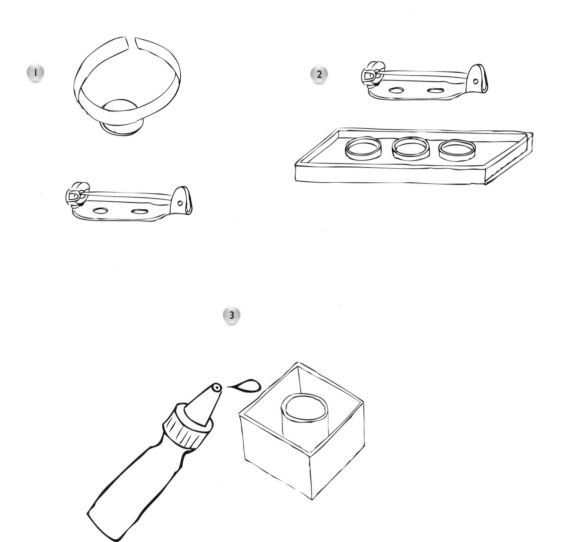

Woven Zigzag Band

This seed-bead wristband means getting handy with some weaving. You can make your own bead-wearing loom and adapt this beautiful zigzag design with your own pattern. Simply plan the pattern out on graph paper first. Stripes can look great, or randomly placed rainbow-coloured beads. You can also experiment with wider and narrower bracelets too.

project by: lisa tilse
suitable for: confident beginners
should take: 2–3 hours

SHOPPING LIST

- 3 to 4 mm glass beads (green, aqua and purple)
- Jewellery thread
- Toggle clasp

CRAFTY NEEDS

- Sewing needle
- Scissors
- Small piece of cardboard (7 × 13 cm)
- Shoe box or large plastic container (30 cm long)
- Blu-Tack
- Masking tape

GET READY

- Gather your tools and materials and clear some space on a sturdy worktable. As you are working with beads and other fiddly bits, you will need to work on a clean space. You may need a towel or felt mat to stop your beads rolling everywhere. Make sure you have a comfy chair and some good lighting too.
- Bead weaving is a popular and addictive pastime. Ordinary sewing thread is not strong enough for this, so make sure you use jewellery thread. Purchase special beading needles from a craft shop, or use an ordinary sewing needle: just make sure your needle has a big enough eye for the jewellery thread, but is narrow enough to pass through your beads.

HOW TO PREPARE YOUR WEAVING LOOM

1. Measure your wrist to work out the length of your bracelet. Make sure it is not a tight fit. Write the measurement down and subtract 4 cm. This will be the length of the woven section of your bracelet.

2. On one long edge of the cardboard piece measure 3.5 cm in from the edge and make nine marks, about 8 mm apart (they don't have to be exact!). Cut slits in the cardboard at each of the nine marks. Tape the card to the short end of your shoe box, so the cut side sticks up over the top by about 1 cm.

3. Cut nine 55 cm lengths of jewellery thread. Knot the threads together and secure them with Blu-Tack to the box below the cardboard piece. Your warp (lengthwise) threads will loosen as you are weaving. It's easier to weave if they are tight, so keep stopping to refix them with the Blu-Tack.

4. Take one thread and bring it up and over the cardboard and through one of the slits. Bring it across the top of the box so it hangs over the other side. Repeat with all the threads – each passing through a different slit. Wrap the threads around a piece of Blu-Tack and secure them to the end of the box so the threads are pulled taut across the top of the box. Now we will create the weft threads that go right to left and start weaving.

HOW TO WEAVE YOUR WEFT THREADS

1. Position the box in front of you so the cardboard piece is furthest away from you. Cut a piece of jewellery thread about 1 metre long and thread your needle. With a double knot, tie the thread onto the first warp thread on the left hand side, about 7 cm in from the top edge of the box.

2. Pass the needle under all nine warp threads. Thread one purple bead and a random selection of seven blue and aqua beads onto the needle (see diagram 2) and push them along to the knot.

3. Hold the weft thread close to the beads with your right hand, and push and hold the beads up between the warp threads with your left index finger (see diagram 3). This is a bit tricky for the first couple of rows, but they will slot easily into place in the rows after that.

4. Working from right to left, pass the needle through the centre of the beads. Make sure you are pushing the beads up between the warp threads so the needle passes over the top of each warp thread (see diagram 4). Pull the weft thread through the beads. Make sure your warp threads are pulled tight each time you change direction.

5. Pass the needle under the warp threads and thread eight more beads on. This row will have two purples and six aqua and greens. Repeat these steps for each row.

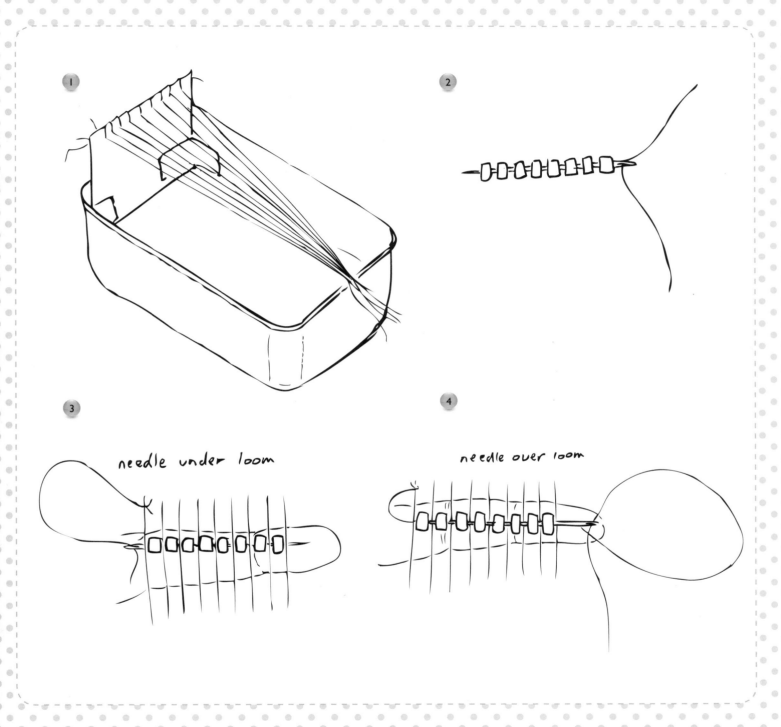

3   needle under loom

4   needle over loom

6. Each row has eight beads on it, in the following pattern:

ROW 1: 1 purple + 7 mixed aqua and green
ROW 2: 2 purple + 6 mixed aqua and green
ROW 3: 3 purple + 5 mixed aqua and green
ROW 4: 4 purple + 4 mixed aqua and green
ROW 5: 5 purple + 3 mixed aqua and green
ROW 6: 6 purple + 2 mixed aqua and green
ROW 7: 5 purple + 3 mixed aqua and green
ROW 8: 4 purple + 4 mixed aqua and green
ROW 9: 3 purple + 5 mixed aqua and green
ROW 10: 2 purple + 6 mixed aqua and green
ROW 11: 1 purple + 7 mixed aqua and green
Repeat from row 1.

7. Check your measurement (loose wrist measurement minus 4 cm), and continue weaving until your bracelet is the correct length (see diagram 5).

HOW TO FINISH YOUR BRACELET

1. Pass the needle and thread back and forth through the previous few rows then cut the thread off as close as you can to the bracelet.

2. Start cutting the warp threads and weaving them into the bracelet in the same way. Starting at the end of the bracelet closest to you, cut warp thread #1 where it passes over the edge of the box and thread it onto the needle. Weave it back and forth through the beads. Then do the same thing with warp thread #9. Cut warp thread #1 at the top of the box and weave it back and forth into that end of the bracelet. Do the same with warp thread #9.

3. Remove the bracelet from the box and the Blu-Tack and cut the knots off the ends of the threads. Warp threads #3 and #7 will not be woven into the bracelet at either end. For all other threads, thread the needle and pass it back down the bracelet parallel to the warp threads. Weave the needle over and under the weft threads as you go.

4. Toward the centre of the bracelet bring the needle up and out (try to do this at a different place in the bracelet for each thread as it is much easier than trying to weave each thread through the same rows). Weave it back and forth through a few rows then cut the thread off close to the last bead. Repeat for each thread at both ends of the bracelet except for threads #3 and #7.

HOW TO ATTACH YOUR CLASP

1. Thread seven green and aqua beads onto thread #3, and four beads onto thread #7. With the needle still threaded onto thread #7, pass the needle through the last three beads on thread #3. Both threads #3 and #7 will now be coming out of the same bead.

2. Pass the two threads in opposite directions through the loop on the toggle clasp and tie a tight double knot. Pass the needle through the last seven beads and then down through the bracelet as before. Thread the needle with the remaining thread and repeat. Finish off the other end of the bracelet with the ring of the toggle clasp in the same way (see diagram 6).

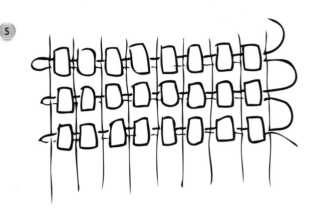

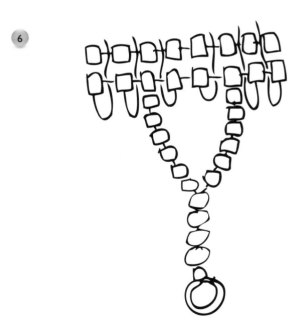

Storm Jewel Set

This storm-inspired ring and brooch motif set is made from shrink plastic sheets, which you can draw or print on, colour in and cut out. All you have to do is heat and shrink them in the oven to make all sorts of cool designs. The motif design works well here as a ring and brooch, but you could make earrings or a pendant if you like too.

project by: kirsty macafee
suitable for: beginners
should take: 1–2 hours

SHOPPING LIST

- Shrink plastic
- Blank ring and brooch findings
- Cotton embroidery thread

CRAFTY NEEDS

- Scissors
- Hole punch
- Jewellery cement glue

GET READY

- Gather your tools and materials and clear some space on a sturdy worktable. As you are working with beads and other fiddly bits, you will need to work on a clean space. For working with glue you should wear protective clothing and when using cement glue, as it can contain toxic fumes. You must work in a well-ventilated space. Read the safe handling of craft tools section on page 17 and be sure to put everything away when you are done.
- You will also be using shrink plastic, which is melted in the oven. Study the instructions on the packet before starting, and read up on pages 11–12 for more information on using this product. You will also be using some jewellery findings, which can be found at bead or craft shops. You can find a description of basic jewellery techniques on pages 13–14.

HOW TO MAKE YOUR SHRINK PLASTIC MOTIFS

1. Draw or trace your design (you can use our designs or create your own) onto the shrink plastic sheet, keeping in mind that your design will shrink to a third of its original size (see diagram 1). Using scissors, cut out your design from the shrink plastic (see diagram 2).

2. Punch any holes you might need at this point, as you won't be able to do this after you have melted it. Place three holes in the bottom of the cloud and one in each of the raindrops, to hang the raindrops from the cloud (see diagram 3). To make a matching pendant you should make a hole through the top of your design that you can thread cord through later.

3. Place your designs onto an oven tray covered in baking paper and melt in the oven according to instructions on your shrink plastic. They need only a few minutes so keep watch. Use heatproof gloves to remove the tray from the oven and let the shrink designs cool before picking them up (see diagram 4).

HOW TO MAKE YOUR JEWELLERY

1. Use embroidery thread or jewellery cord to attach any loose elements to your design – such as the raindrops to the cloud. Knot your thread onto the raindrops and then onto the back of the cloud for the brooch design.

2. Use jewellery cement glue (or a hot glue gun) to attach your shrink design onto your ring or badge back. For your badge, catch all the loose strings from your knots into the glue at the back to secure them in place (see diagram 5).

Pizzazz Hair Ribbon

Grab some pretty ribbon and a few sparkly beads and you can make a headband to add some pizzazz to your hairdo! Try mixing it up by changing the ribbon colour and beads. You'll soon be designing your own fabulous headbands.

project by: lisa tilse

suitable for: confident beginner

should take: 1–2 hours

SHOPPING LIST

- Sturdy cotton ribbon (such as grosgrain ribbon) or bias tape (12 mm wide) in any colour you like
- 7 cm length of 10–12 mm wide elastic (to coordinate with your ribbon)
- Sewing thread
- Small sparkly and/or cute beads
- Shiny seed beads

CRAFTY NEEDS

- Tape measure
- Sewing machine or hand-sewing kit
- Scissors
- Pins

GET READY

- Gather your tools and materials and clear some space on a sturdy worktable. As you are working with beads and other fiddly bits, you will need to work on a clean space. You may need a towel or felt mat to stop your beads rolling everywhere. Make sure you have a comfy chair and some good lighting too.
- This project requires some simple sewing. Don't worry if you have never sewn before, your stitches won't need to be perfect. For hand sewing you will need a basic sewing kit (page 8) to get started.

HOW TO MAKE YOUR BAND

1. Wrap your ribbon around your head to check for the correct size. It should be a comfortable fit – not too tight and not loose. The ends of the ribbon should meet but not overlap. Cut the ribbon.

2. Cut 8 cm off the ribbon and pin one end to your elastic. The right side of the ribbon should be facing toward the elastic.

3. Machine or hand-sew the ribbon to the elastic and leave a 5 mm seam allowance. Stitch back and forth a few times for added strength. Fold the ribbon up and over the stitched line and sew another line of stitches a couple of millimetres above the previous line (see diagram 1).

4. Try your headband on again. Stretch the elastic to meet the ribbon and overlap it slightly (to allow for the seam you will sew next). If it's too loose, trim a small amount off the ribbon and test the fit again. When you are happy with the fit, sew the other end of the ribbon onto the other end of the elastic as before. Use pins to mark the top middle section of your headband, where you want your beads to go.

HOW TO MAKE YOUR BEADED DESIGN

1. Lay your headband on your work surface. Using the pattern as a guide, create your design, or even place the beads completely at random.

2. Choose a needle and thread that will go through your bead hole. Using a double thread with a knot tied in the end, start at one end of your marked area with a small double stitch. Sew the larger beads in place first: Sew through each bead two to three times to make sure it is securely attached. Finish with your needle pulled through to the back of the ribbon.

3. Work out the positioning of the next bead and bring your needle up through the front of the ribbon in the spot where the bead will go, then sew in place. Continue like this until you have sewn on all the large beads.

4. Start back at the beginning and sew on the seed beads. Sew them on in the same way as the larger beads, but thread three to four beads onto your needle at once (see diagrams 2 and 3).

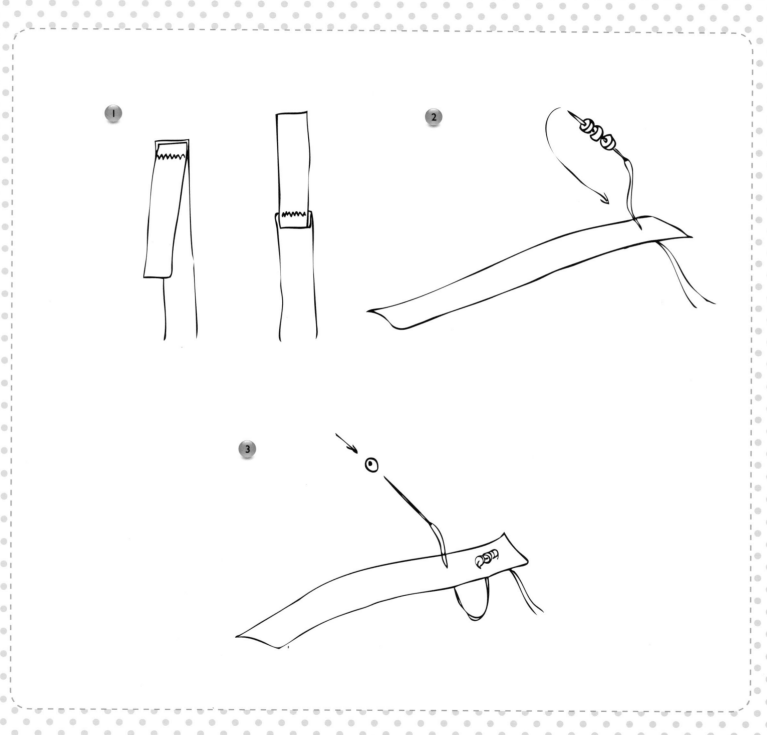

DIY Badge

Everybody should have a batch of badges to pin to their hat, bag or jacket. Personalise your collection by making your own DIY (design it yourself) badges to add to the mix. These badges are super simple to make – with glue, leather and few beads you are set to go.

project by: kirsty macafee

suitable for: confident beginners

should take: 1–2 hours

SHOPPING LIST

- Leather or faux leather off-cuts
- Craft felt
- Seed beads and bugle beads
- Cotton thread
- Metal charms or buttons
- Badge back

CRAFTY NEEDS

- Jewellery glue
- Scissors
- Needle and thread

GET READY

- Gather your tools and materials and clear some space on a sturdy worktable.

As you are working with beads and other fiddly bits, you will need to work on a clean space. For working with glue you should wear protective clothing and cover your workspace with newspaper. You may need a towel or felt mat to stop your beads rolling everywhere. Make sure you have a comfy chair and some good lighting too.

- You will be using a strong, all-purpose cement glue for this project. Take care as it can give off toxic fumes. You must work in a well-ventilated space. Read the safe handling of craft tools section on page 17 and be sure to put everything away when you are done.
- This project requires some simple sewing. For hand sewing you will need a basic sewing kit (page 8) to get started.

HOW TO MAKE YOUR DESIGN

1. To the make the badges use leather off-cuts, which you can find at a fabric or craft store, but if you can't get hold of any try using faux leather, craft felt or even faux vinyl off-cuts from a hardware store.

2. Create your own design or use the badge or flower design provided here (see diagram 1), drawing it onto paper to make a template. Cut out your design in two contrasting colours or materials, using your leather, faux leather or craft felt (or a combination of these).

3. Decide which material or colour will be your base and which will be your accent. Place your drawing over the accent piece and cut away sections of your accent colour so that the base colour peeks through (see diagram 2).

HOW TO MAKE YOUR BEADED BADGES

1. For the flower badge, first layer your base and accent pieces and run a line of all-purpose glue around the underside of your accent colour and attach it to the base piece. Cut a piece of beading thread and tie a knot in one end. Thread the needle and bring the thread up from the back of the flower to the front near the centre (see diagram 3).

2. Place 10 seed beads onto the thread then take the needle back through the base to make a loop of beads. Repeat once for each petal. Sew or glue a contrasting button into the flower centre (see diagram 4).

3. Use jewellery glue or your hot glue gun to attach the brooch back onto your badges. If you don't have a brooch back you can stitch on a safety pin instead.

nifty necklaces

You can never have too many necklaces! *This section shows you how to make four gorgeous necklaces that will make any outfit a winner. There's a super-colourful necklace made with ribbons and beads, a sweet bunting necklace, a cool collaged necklace, or the blingy Aztec Garden Neckband if you really want to stand out. You can make these necklaces in different colours to match different outfits, or make them for your friends and family members.*

None of these necklaces are very difficult to make, although some designs might take a bit more patience than others. If you aren't sure about anything, read the techniques section first and ask for help if you need it. And don't worry if your necklace isn't perfect first time around — just make another one! You'll become a pro in no time, and will be able to show all of your friends how to make them too!

Bunting Chain

Clash Collage

Fragment Fancy

Aztec Garden Neckband

Bunting Chain

Bunting can be a string of flags or a festive decoration, in a gentle row. Make this mini set of bunting from painted leather and wear it as a necklace, or make a slightly longer one to string up in your room. The technique you will learn here is so versatile you will be making lots of these designs to give to all your friends.

project by: lisa tilse
suitable for: beginners
should take: 1–2 hours

SHOPPING LIST

- Light coloured leather or vinyl scraps (25 × 5 cm piece, or lots of scraps)
- Acrylic paint
- Jewellery cord, waxed cotton or faux leather cord
- 10 silver jump rings
- 20 cm lengths of 3 mm wide ribbon in 3 different colours

CRAFTY NEEDS

- Large embroidery needle, or an awl
- Small pliers or tweezers
- Scissors
- Pen
- Ruler
- Paintbrush
- Plastic tray or lid to mix paint on
- Plastic cup

GET READY

- Gather your tools and materials and clear some space on a sturdy worktable. As you are working with beads and other fiddly bits, you will need to work on a clean space. For working with glue you should wear protective clothing and cover your workspace with newspaper. You may need a towel or felt mat to stop your beads rolling everywhere. Make sure you have a comfy chair and some good lighting too.
- You will be using some jewellery findings, which can be found at bead or craft shops. You can find a description of basic jewellery techniques on pages 13–14.
- You will also be experimenting with mixing paint colours. Use a plastic tray to mix your paint colours. You can easily mix your own if you don't have pastel colours on hand.
- Pastel pink: a small amount of red and lots of white
- Pale lavender: a small amount of blue and red, and lots of white
- Pale aqua: small amounts of blue and green, and lots of white
- Pale mint: small amounts of blue and yellow, and lots of white

HOW TO MAKE YOUR BUNTING FLAGS

1. On the back of your vinyl or leather pieces draw a rectangle 3 x 25 cm. On the top line mark intervals of 2.5 cm and on the bottom line first measure in 1.25 cm then mark intervals of 2.5 cm. Join the marks diagonally to create a zigzag (see diagram 1). Cut along both long sides of the rectangle, and then cut along the diagonal lines to create the bunting triangles (see diagram 2).

2. Paint the right sides of the each of the triangles with a different colour. You will only need eight for this necklace, so you will have lots of spares to make extras for your friends. Experiment with painting stripes or spots on some. Set aside to dry.

3. Choose which eight triangles you will use for this necklace then lay them out in order in front of you on top of a felt sheet or piece of thick cardboard. Use a large embroidery needle (or an awl) to poke a hole a couple of millimetres in from the top two corners of each triangle (see diagram 3).

HOW TO MAKE YOUR NECKLACE

1. Connect the bunting triangles together with 3 jump rings (see diagram 4). First open up the rings using your pliers and feed one through each of the holes you made in the triangles. Close the jump rings again with your pliers. Attach the jump rings together using a third jump ring in the centre. Add another jump ring to the last two flags on either end.

2. Cut two 72 cm lengths of jewellery cord. Fold one of the pieces in half and thread the folded end 1 cm through the end jump ring of your bunting chain. Thread both the ends through the loop and pull the knot tight. Do the same with the other cord on the other end of the bunting chain. Tie a knot in the double cord about 17 cm up and also in the end, to keep the two cords together. Repeat with the other side.

3. Take the three lengths of pastel ribbon and trim the ends on the diagonal (to prevent them from fraying). Fold the three ribbons over together, but not in half – the ends should be different lengths. Thread the loops together through the centre jump ring between the last two triangles. Feed all the ribbon ends through the loop and pull the knot tight.

3. To wear, just tie the ends of the cord together behind your neck.

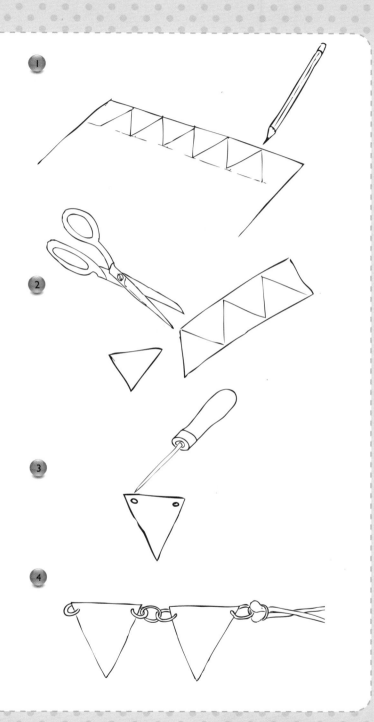

Clash Collage

Did you know that you can design your own beads with collage? The collaged beads look wonderful in bright colours and clashing patterns. Go crazy with this! Some glue, wooden beads and pretty scraps of fabric are all you need for this project. You will be making this necklace in two stages, as the collage beads need to be made a day ahead.

project by: nanette louchart-fletcher
suitable for: beginners
should take: 1–2 hours

SHOPPING LIST

- Small scraps of 6 different fabrics (5 mm pieces and smaller)
- Wooden beads (big and medium)
- 4 strips of torn fabric (each 5 mm × 40 cm)
- Acrylic paints

CRAFTY NEEDS

- PVA craft glue
- Embroidery needle
- Sewing machine or hand-sewing kit
- Old plastic container (for the glue)
- Scissors
- Paintbrush
- Pins

GET READY

- Gather your tools and materials and clear some space on a sturdy worktable. As you are working with beads and other fiddly bits, you will need to work on a clean space. For working with glue you should wear protective clothing and cover your workspace with newspaper. Things can get a big icky with this project! You may need a towel or felt mat to stop your beads rolling everywhere. Make sure you have a comfy chair and some good lighting too.
- This project requires some simple sewing. Don't worry if you have never sewn before, your stitches won't need to be perfect. For hand sewing you will need a basic sewing kit (page 8) to get started.

HOW TO MAKE YOUR COLLAGED BEADS

1. Mix a little water with your glue – just a few drops, to lighten the texture – then drop a couple of the scraps of fabric into the glue. Soak the entire surface of the fabric in glue, both front and back. Take each piece and carefully apply it to the surface of your wooden bead, using your paintbrush or your finger to smooth the surface of the fabric so that it sits completely flat without creases (see diagram 1). Slightly overlap each piece of fabric as you apply it to the bead. Continue until the bead is completely covered, leaving the holes free to string the thread.

2. If you don't have any brightly coloured wooden beads, you can create some by painting your spare plain wooden beads in pretty matching colours using acrylic paints. Leave your beads to dry overnight before you go on to the next stage of the project.

HOW TO MAKE YOUR NECKLACE

1. Take your fabric-collaged beads and your painted beads and lay out your design idea on a felt mat, as if you were about to start threading. Play around with the arrangement of the beads until you find the pattern you like best.

2. Take one long, thin strip of torn fabric and thread it through the eye of your large embroidery needle. Working from one end, thread on a bead at a time. Make sure you follow the order of your pattern. Put a knot in the fabric strip between each bead as you go, to create a little space in between (see diagram 2). Once you have strung all your beads onto the fabric put it to one side.

3. Take the three remaining torn strips of fabric and knot them together at one end. Starting from the tip of the knot, tightly plait the fabric until you are happy with the length (see diagram 3). Check that the necklace will slip comfortably over your head, as there is no clasp. Once you are happy with the length, knot the other end of the plaited fabric.

4. Pin the plaited fabric ends to the beaded fabric ends to form a full necklace. Using a sewing machine (or you can hand-sew if you like), sew back and forth across the join on both sides of the necklace, as shown in diagram 4. (If hand sewing be sure to make strong stitches so it doesn't come undone.) Trim your threads and wear your design proudly.

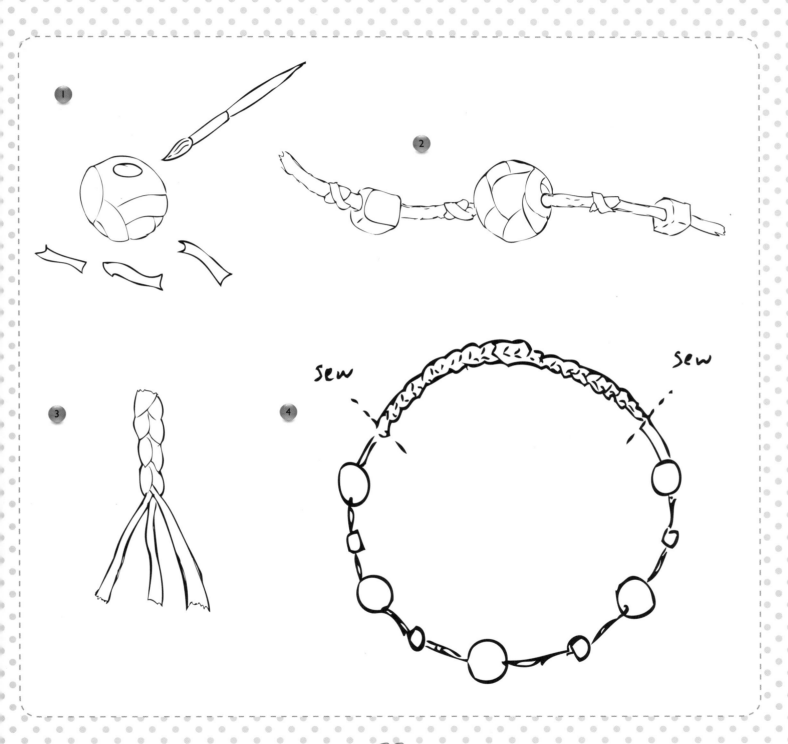

Fragment Fancy

Pieces of ribbon or scraps and fragments of fabric, a couple of interesting beads, needle and thread are all you need to make one of these fancy necklaces. Make one to match every outfit, as a birthday present for your best friend or to surprise your mum or your favourite teacher! They're fun to make and even more fun to wear!

project by: pascale mestdagh
suitable for: confident beginners
should take: 2–3 hours

SHOPPING LIST

- 25 cm length of 2.5 cm wide cotton ribbon (such as grosgrain ribbon) or 50 cm strip of fabric
- 50 cm length of 1.25 cm wide cotton twill tape
- Small scraps of cotton fabric for flower (for variation 3)
- Assorted beads and embellishments
- 25 cm length of 1 cm wide satin ribbon (for variation 2)

CRAFTY NEEDS

- Needle, scissors and measuring tape
- Embroidery thread and sewing thread to match your ribbon

GET READY

- Gather your tools and materials and clear some space on a sturdy worktable. As you are working with beads and other fiddly bits, you will need to work on a clean space. This project requires some simple sewing. Don't worry if you have never sewn before, your stitches won't need to be perfect. For hand sewing you will need a basic sewing kit (page 8) to get started. You may need a towel or felt mat to stop your beads rolling everywhere. Make sure you have a comfy chair and some good lighting too.

HOW TO MAKE YOUR RIBBON NECKLACE

1. Lay your 2.5 cm wide ribbon out in front of you. Thread an embroidery needle with embroidery thread and knot the end. Make your first tiny stitch 3 cm from one side, centred at the middle of the ribbon. Take one big stitch (1.5 cm long) and pull the thread. Push the ribbon with your finger at the same time to make the first pleat.

2. Slip the first bead onto your needle and push it all the way up the thread and against the first pleat (see diagram 1). Make the next pleat, by making another stitch and push the ribbon against the first bead (see diagram 2).

3. Slip the next bead onto the needle and proceed as in the previous steps until all the beads have been sewn into place. Finish with a last pleat. Sew once more through all pleats and beads with your needle and thread to secure. Fasten off and trim your thread at the back.

4. Fold over the ends of the ribbon (about 1 cm) towards the back. Take your twill tape and position it against the fold at the back. Sew into place with a couple of stitches through all three layers (folded ribbon and twill tape, see diagram 3). Repeat at the other end, but first test that the necklace will fit over your head… Done!

VARIATION 2 : SPOTTED RIBBON NECKLACE

1. Lay the 1 cm wide satin ribbon along the centre of the wider ribbon and sew down the centre through both layers. You can add a seed bead between each pleat or just gather up the fabric in small pleats. Finish the necklace as before.

VARIATION 3 : RUFFLED FABRIC NECKLACE

1. Place a 50 cm strip of torn fabric in front of you and thread your needle with embroidery thread. Starting 3 cm from the side, make small running stitches in a straight line centred along the middle line to ruffle your fabric. Stop stitches 3 cm from the other end. Hold onto the thread and pull against the fabric so that the fabric starts to ruffle (see diagram 4). Make a fabric ruffle strip that is 25 cm long. Fasten the thread in the back with a couple of stitches and a knot.

2. Pleat the ruffled strip as explained in version 1, starting with one pleat and slipping on a bead, then making another pleat. Do this for three beads then sew back through the pleats and beads to secure them. Fasten off and repeat the process at the other end with two beads.

3. Cut three circles from different coloured fabrics, each slightly bigger than the next (approx 5 cm diameter). Place the circles on top of each other, the smallest one on top, and the biggest one on the bottom. Thread a needle with embroidery floss.

From the back, pull the thread through the centre and make a small stitch. Slightly fold the circle and make a couple of stitches in the back to form a flower.

4. Slip a small bead onto your needle and sew onto the centre of the flower. Repeat this process with two more beads (see diagram 5). Place the flower on your ruffled fabric strip, positioning it in one side, and secure it with a couple of stitches.

5. Attach the twill tape as explained in version 1, add sequins and bright and shiny gemstones.

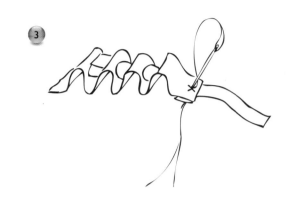

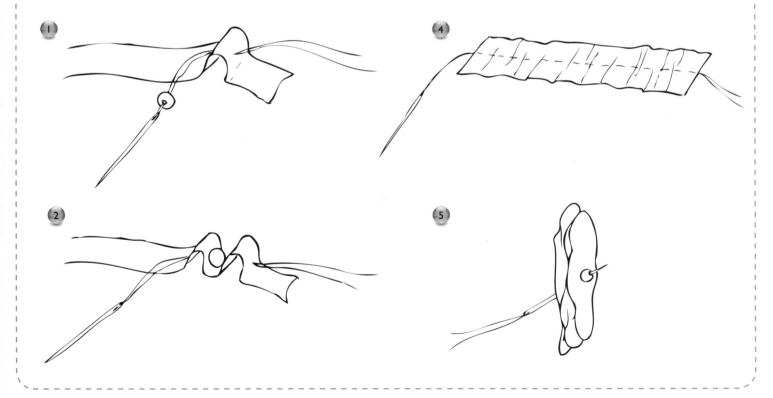

Aztec Garden Neckband

Add some bling to your outfit the next time you go out with friends with this trendy bib-style neckband. Take some fabric and sew on bright and sparkly beads in this Aztec inspired design. If you don't want another necklace you can change the shape of your fabric base to made a headband or armband.

project by: kathreen ricketson
suitable for: confident beginners
should take: 2–3 hours

SHOPPING LIST

- 5 sparkly buttons or flat beads
- 20 long bugle beads
- 20 short bugle beads
- 20 seed beads
- Felt fabric
- Chain
- Ribbon

CRAFTY NEEDS

- Beading needle
- Sewing thread
- Spray glue

GET READY

- Gather your tools and materials and clear some space on a sturdy worktable. As you are working with beads and other fiddly bits, you will need to work on a clean space. For working with glue you should wear protective clothing and cover your workspace with newspaper. You may need a towel or felt mat to stop your beads rolling everywhere. Make sure you have a comfy chair and some good lighting too.
- This project requires some simple sewing. For hand sewing you will need a basic sewing kit (page 8) to get started.
- You will also need a beading needle, or use a regular small sewing needle but check first that it will thread through the hole in your smallest bead.

HOW TO MAKE

1. Cut your piece of felt into a crescent moon shape for a necklace or a rectangle (5 x 15 cm) for a headband or armband. Choose your beads, and lay them out onto a spare piece of felt in your chosen design – you can either make up your own design, place them at random or follow the design shown here. Mark lightly in pencil onto your base fabric where you will be placing the main parts of your design.

2. Thread your needle with 60 cm of sewing cotton, double it and knot in the end. Starting in the centre of your design, bring the needle up from the back, and thread on your first bead (see diagram 1). Push the needle back down through the fabric. For large beads, thread your needle through 2 to 3 times per bead but for seed beads and sequins once will be enough. Bring the needle back up again where the next bead will go. Thread the bead onto the needle, and place the bead into position. Push the needle back down through the fabric to secure the bead in place. Continue using your beads in this way.

3. Sew a row of bugle beads parallel to the edges of your base fabric (see diagram 2).

4. For the edging, bring the needle through the material from the back and thread three beads onto your needle in their correct order (see diagram 3). Push the needle back through the fabric ensuring that the beads are correctly placed.

5. Add some seed beads in the same way in a random design if you like. Tie off all the threads at the back.

6. For the necklace, sew each end of a small chain of links onto both ends of the fabric (see diagram 4) and then tie a ribbon onto each end of the chain as your necklace tie. For the armband or headband, sew a strip of ribbon to each end of your beaded piece. If you want to hide all the unsightly knots and threads at the back, you could layer another piece of fabric or felt at the back and attach with glue, then sew a running stitch around the outside to secure it in place.

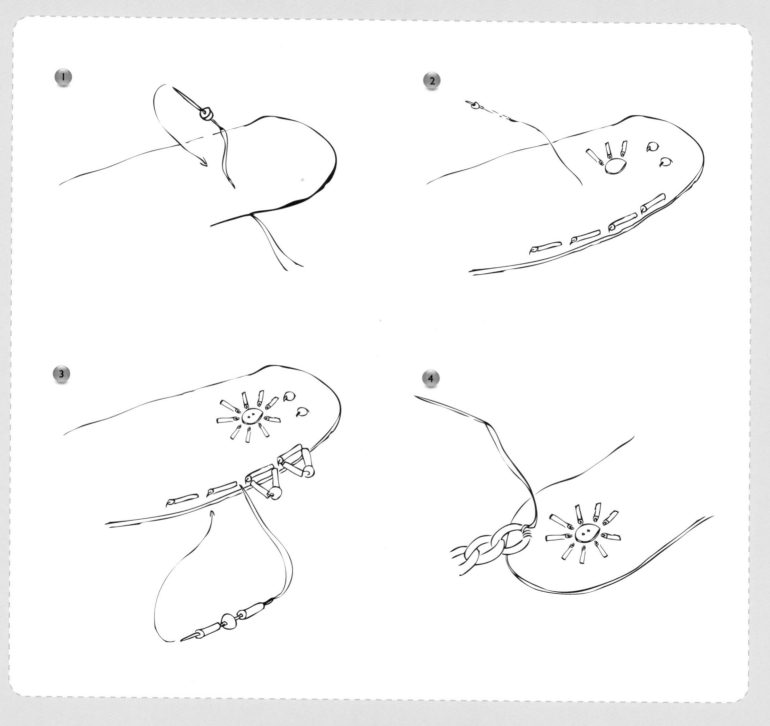

spruce your space

Deck out your room in your own personal style. *Add some creative colour and sparkle to jazz up your space. Beaded ornaments, a button wall hanging, nature door curtain or a fuse bead Ghostie Garland, are just a few of the ideas in this chapter for both boys and girls. Whatever your taste, you will find something here to reproduce or remix. Have a go today!*

The projects in this section range from super easy to a bit trickier. None of them are very difficult, although some designs might take a bit more patience than others. Some projects require a hot glue gun or a needle and thread. If you aren't sure about anything read the techniques section first and ask for help if you need it. Don't fuss about perfection, the aim is to be creative, make something cool and enjoy the process. Nab a plate of something yummy, grab your iPod and start sprucing!

Ghostie Garland

Gamer Magnets

Push Button Canvas

Freckles Photo Frame

Crazy Critters

Beachy Wind Chime

Twinkle Ornament

Pentagram Web Sun Catcher

A Seaside Treasury

Ghostie Garland

Fuse beads are so much fun to play with. You can make lots of different motifs by fusing these colourful plastic beads together with an iron. Once you make your motifs you can do all sorts of things with them. Here we have strung them up to make a cool garland for your room.

project by: kathreen ricketson
suitable for: beginners
should take: less than 1 hour

SHOPPING LIST

- Fuse beads and pegboard
- Jewellery thread or embroidery thread

CRAFTY NEEDS

- Iron
- Baking paper
- Embroidery or jewellery needle

GET READY

- Gather your tools and materials and clear some space on a sturdy worktable. As you are working with beads and other fiddly bits, you will need to work on a clean space. You may need a towel or felt mat to stop your beads rolling everywhere. Make sure you have a comfy chair and some good lighting too.
- Take care when using an iron, as it can cause burns. Read the safe handling of craft tools section on page 17 and be sure to put everything away when you are done.
- Here you will be using fuse beads, which are fused together with an iron. Read the instructions on the packet as well as the information about fuse beads on page 11 before starting.

HOW TO MAKE

1. Lay out your fuse beads on your pegboard in the formation shown in diagram 1. Put your iron on to warm up.

2. Cover your bead design with a piece of baking paper and gently rub your hot iron back and forth over it so the beads melt slightly and fuse together.

3. Wait for your design to cool down before removing it from the pegboard. Turn it over and cover with the baking paper and again gently iron it.

4. Make about 10 to 15 of these little ghostie dudes. Take your needle and embroidery thread and string through the top holes of each ghost (see diagram 2). Create a loop in both ends of your thread and hang the string of ghosts across your room.

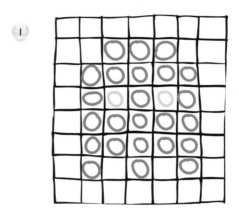

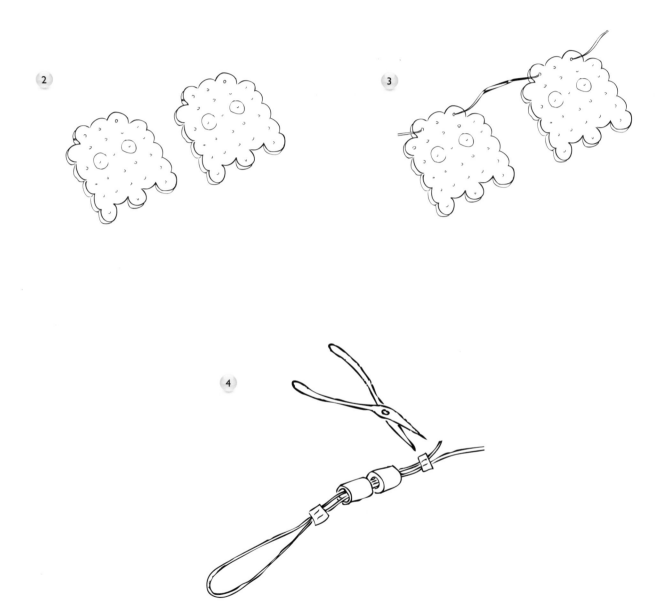

Gamer Magnets

Take your colourful fuse beads, an iron and lots of imagination and turn them into nerdy gamer-style magnets. Make your favourite Nintendo or other computer-game-inspired shapes and display them on any metal surface.

project by: lisa tilse
suitable for: beginners
should take: 1–2 hours

SHOPPING LIST

- Fuse beads and pegboard
- Magnet tape (or small magnets and jewellery cement glue)

CRAFTY NEEDS

- Jewellery cement glue
- Iron
- Baking paper

GET READY

- Gather your tools and materials and clear some space on a sturdy worktable. As you are working with beads and other fiddly bits, you will need to work on a clean space. For working with glue you should wear protective clothing and cover your workspace with newspaper. You may need a towel or felt mat to stop your beads rolling everywhere. Make sure you have a comfy chair and some good lighting too.
- Here you will be using fuse beads, which are fused together with an iron. Be sure to read the instructions on page 11 and on the packet before starting. Take care when using an iron, as it can cause burns. Read the safe handling of craft tools section on page 17 and be sure to put everything away when you are done.

HOW TO MAKE

1. Use the patterns supplied, or create your own game characters and consoles by placing fuse beads into position on your pegboard. Cover your creation with a piece of baking paper and gently rub the iron back and forth over it so the beads melt slightly and fuse together.

2. When it has cooled remove the character from the base. Turn your design over and place the baking paper on top and gently iron it again.

3. Cut a piece of self-adhesive magnet tape and attach it to the back of your character, or use jewellery cement glue to attach a regular magnet in place.

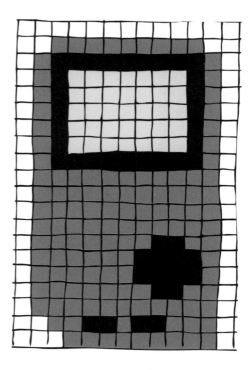

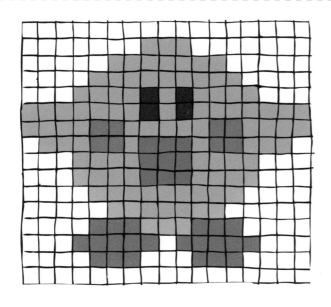

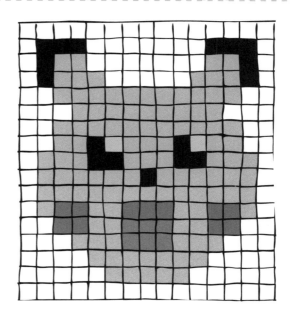

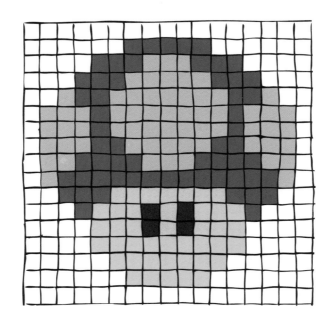

Push Button Canvas

Brighten up your walls with these personalised wall hangings made from colourful buttons. You can use recycled buttons, vintage or new. Buttons come in all sorts of wonderful colours, textures and sizes and are perfect for this project. You will need a canvas frame, your button collection and a hot glue gun. Get ready, it is going to be lots of fun!

project by: nicole vaughan
suitable for: beginners
should take: 1–3 hours

SHOPPING LIST

• Square mounted canvas (about 145 mm square and 38 mm deep)
• Buttons

CRAFTY NEEDS

• Hot glue gun
• Pencil and eraser

GET READY

• Gather your tools and materials and clear some space on a sturdy worktable. As you are working with beads and other fiddly bits, you will need to work on a clean space. For working with glue you should wear protective clothing and cover your workspace with newspaper. Make sure you have a comfy chair and some good lighting too.

• Take care when using a hot glue gun as they can give off toxic fumes. You must work in a well-ventilated space. Read the safe handling of craft tools section on page 17 and be sure to put everything away when you are done.

HOW TO MAKE

1. Lightly sketch the alphabet letter, or outline of your design, onto your canvas. Have a play with your buttons on the canvas to work out your design. Turn on your hot glue gun to warm it up.

2. Once your glue is ready to use, glue your buttons onto the outline of your drawn design (see diagram 1). Start placing the larger buttons first. Decide where you want to place your first button and put a dab of hot glue on to the frame and push your button down. Be careful when pushing down that you don't put your fingers over the buttonholes as glue will come through these and could burn you. You'll have to work quite quickly so the hot glue doesn't go cold. If it does go cold, you should be able to carefully pull the glue off and try again.

3. Keep on gluing buttons onto the canvas until you're happy with how it's looking. Add a button frame around your design and on the deep sides of your canvas. Start with gluing the four largest buttons to each front corner of your canvas, then glue filler buttons in between to frame your design (see diagram 2).

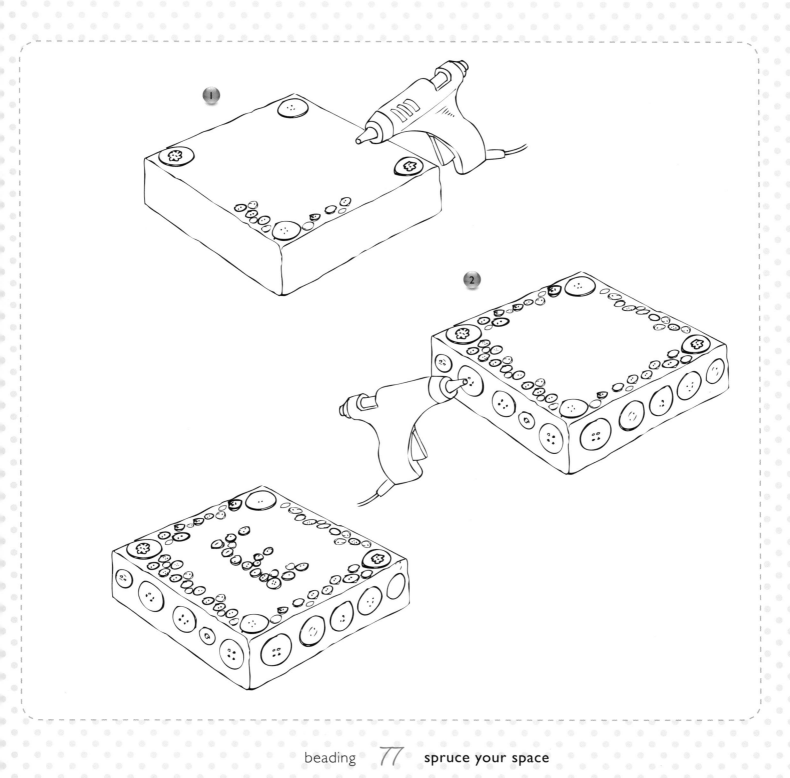

Freckles Photo Frame

These easy photo frames are a fun way to show off your fave photos. You don't need to buy photo frames; you can make your own with cardboard and beads. Make a beach-inspired design with plain wooden beads, or a bright cheerful freckly version with sparkly and freckly fun beads.

project by: lisa tilse
suitable for: beginners
should take: 2–3 hours

SHOPPING LIST

• Stiff cardboard
• Beads

CRAFTY NEEDS

• Craft knife and cutting mat
• Pencil
• Ruler
• Hot glue gun or cement glue
• Paper masking tape

GET READY

• Gather your tools and materials and clear some space on a sturdy worktable. As you are working with beads and other fiddly bits, you will need to work on a clean space. For working with glue you should wear protective clothing and cover your workspace with newspaper. You may need a towel or felt mat to stop your beads rolling everywhere. Make sure you have a comfy chair and some good lighting too.

• Take care when using a hot glue gun as they can give off toxic fumes. You must work in a well-ventilated space.

• When using a craft knife never press too hard, as there is more chance of losing control of the knife and ruining your project or cutting yourself. To cut through cardboard make a number of light cuts in the same place. Read the safe handling of craft tools section on page 17 and be sure to put everything away when you are done.

HOW TO MAKE YOUR TEMPLATE

1. Round frame: Find two round objects, such as small bowls and cups, to trace around. Place the larger object on the cardboard and trace around it. Centre the smaller object within the outer circle and trace around it too. Place the cardboard on your cutting mat and carefully cut around the circles using your craft knife.

2. Rectangular frame: Place your cardboard on the cutting mat and draw two rectangles that measure 18 x 14.5 cm. Cut the rectangles out with a craft knife and ruler or your scissors. Take one cardboard rectangle and draw a line parallel to each edge, 3.5 cm in. Using your craft knife and a ruler, cut out the centre rectangle. Place the tip of your craft knife in the corner and cut away from the corner halfway along the line and stop (see diagram 1). Then turn the cardboard around and place the tip of your knife in the next corner. Cut away from the corner again until the two cuts join.

HOW TO ATTACH YOUR BEADS

1. If you are using a hot glue gun, plug it in to warm up. The hot glue tends to set fairly quickly so work on small areas at a time.

2. Choose your beads. On the round frame a mixture of medium multi-coloured plastic pony beads and smaller seed beads were used and on the rectangular frame, 12 mm white and natural wooden beads were used.

3. For the rectangular frame, place the beads in rows. Apply a 3–4 cm strip of glue on the outer edge of the frame then place a row of beads along the glued edge. Apply another small section of glue and place more beads on top (see diagram 2). Repeat the process until you have covered your frame with beads.

4. For the round frame mix the beads together in a small bowl. Cover a 2 cm square section of the frame in a thick layer of glue, tip some seed beads over the glue and press with your finger. Continue covering small areas until your frame is complete. Tip the frame upside down over a bowl to get rid of any loose beads.

HOW TO FINISH YOUR FRAME

1. Round frame: Measure the hole in the centre of your frame and print your favourite photo to fit. Attach your photo to the back of your frame with tape.

2. Rectangular frame: Lay the beaded frame face down. Place the second cardboard rectangle next to it (see diagram 3). Butt the two pieces together and tape along the join with masking tape. Trim both ends of the tape flush with the edges of the frame. The frame will stand up in an upside-down V shape.

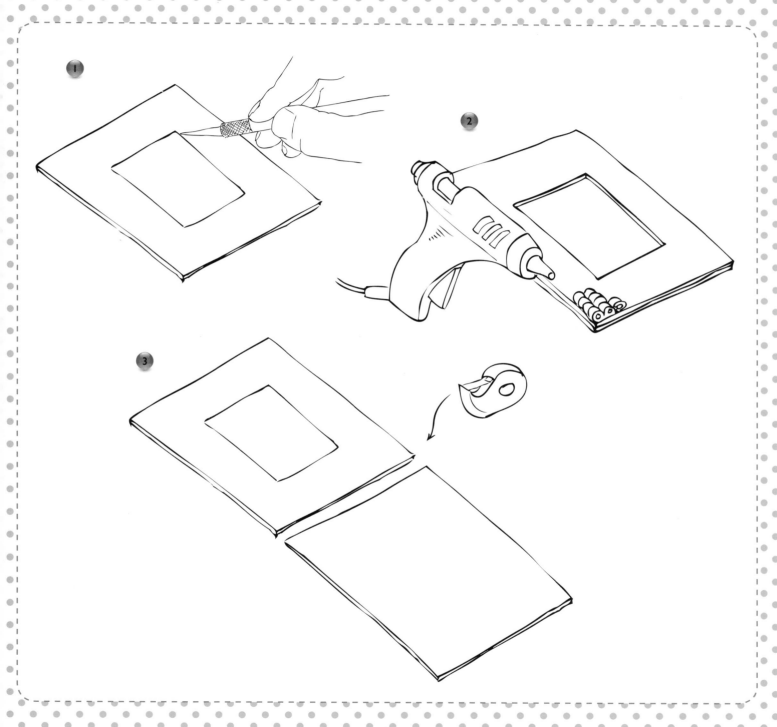

Crazy Critters

With a few beads, some cord or string and your imagination, you can make a whole menagerie of critter friends. Follow the directions here to make your own insect-inspired creations: once you get the hang of this technique you will be creating your own designs in no time. Display them on your windowsill, or hang them from your ceiling!

project by: nicole vaughan
suitable for: confident beginners
should take: 2–3 hours

SHOPPING LIST

- Plastic or glass pony beads
- 50 cm length of 0.5 to 1 mm wide waxed cotton or leather cord (check that it will fit through your beads at least twice)

GET READY

- Gather your tools and materials and clear some space on a sturdy worktable. As you are working with beads and other fiddly bits, you will need to work on a clean space. You may need a towel or felt mat to stop your beads rolling everywhere. Make sure you have a comfy chair and some good lighting too.
- The instructions here show you how to make the basic critter body shape, as well as how to vary the body shape by adding more rows of beads for extra length and adding more beads to each row to make the body more rotund. Options are also given here to add wings, legs, tails and antennae.

HOW TO MAKE

1. Take a 50 cm length of cord and find the centre point. Thread the first bead down to the centre and lay out your cord in front of you with the bead furthest away (see diagram 1).

2. To make the basic body shape, take the right end of the cord and thread on the second row of beads, and take the left end of the cord and thread them through the opposite side of these beads (see diagram 2).

3. Take the right side cord and thread the third row of beads, and then take the left side cord and thread it through the other side of each of these beads (see diagram 3). Continue in this way to create a basic body shape, following diagram 4. At any time you can add a wing. To finish you can add a tail.

4. To create the wings, take the right side cord and thread on three beads, then thread this back through the second and first bead and pull tight. For an extra wing repeat this step with another three beads. Repeat for the other side of the cord.

5. To make the tail, thread three beads onto the ends of both cords from the same direction. To make a longer tail, just add another bead or two. To finish take one of the cords and thread it back through the last bead, pull tight and knot to finish.

6. To add the legs and antennae use a piece of cord 20 cm long. Thread it through the row of beads where you want the legs. Tie a knot at one end, leaving a length of cord that will be the leg, and do the same for other end. Trim your legs to the same length. Add cord in the same way, coming out of the top bead for your antennae.

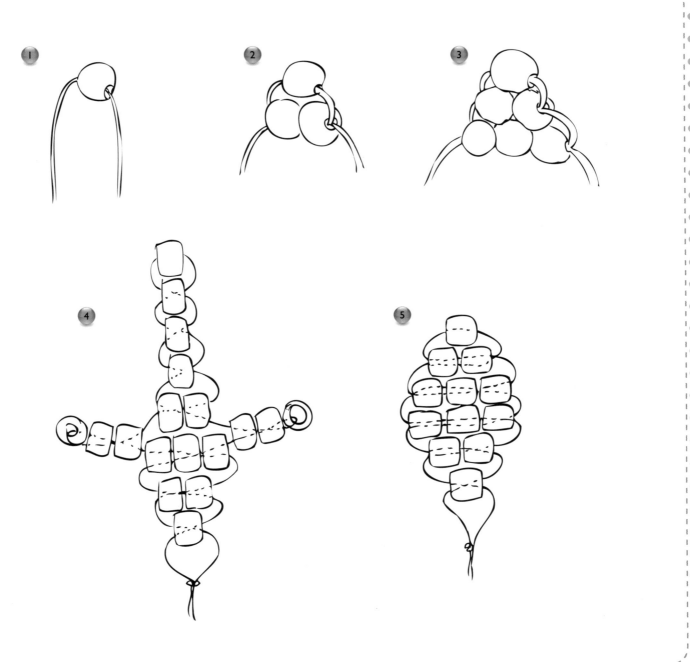

Beachy Wind Chime

This beach-inspired wind chime is perfect to hang somewhere that catches a little breeze, near your window or outside under the eaves. Collect shells and glass worn smooth by the waves when you are next at the beach, or even smooth pebbles would do. Create visual interest with different sizes, textures and colours.

project by: lisa tilse
suitable for: confident beginners
should take: 1–2 hours

SHOPPING LIST

- Assorted glass and natural beads
- Found objects like glass or china pieces worn smooth by the ocean or else shells or smooth flat pebbles
- Two small found sticks (25 to 30 cm long)
- Jewellery wire (18 to 24 gauge)
- Jewellery thread

CRAFTY NEEDS

- Pliers
- Wire cutters

GET READY

- Gather your tools and materials and clear some space on a sturdy worktable. As you are working with beads and other fiddly bits, you will need to work on a clean space. You may need a towel or felt mat to stop your beads rolling everywhere. Make sure you have a comfy chair and some good lighting too.
- Here you will be using pliers and wire to twist around beads. This is not tricky, but you can find a description of basic jewellery techniques on pages 13–14. Read the safe handling of craft tools section on page 17 and be sure to put everything away when you are done.

HOW TO PREPARE YOUR FOUND OBJECTS

1. Take your beach glass, pottery shards or smooth pebbles and, as these do not have holes in them, wrap jewellery wire around each piece.

2. Use your wire cutters to cut a length of wire about 70 cm long. Fold the wire in half. Thread a small bead onto the wire and position it at the halfway point (see diagram 1). Thread both ends of the wire through a bigger bead and pull the bead down until it sits on top of the first bead (see diagram 2).

3. Lay the piece of glass next to the bead and between the two lengths of wire. Wrap the two pieces of wire around the glass a couple of times from top to bottom in opposite directions (see diagram 3). Make sure that the wire is wrapped tightly so the glass can't fall out. Bring the two lengths of wire together at the top of the glass and twist them tightly around each other to secure the glass.

HOW TO MAKE YOUR DROPS

1. Thread both pieces of wire through a random selection of beads until you've reached a drop length of 25 cm, then set it aside. Create visual interest by varying the size, shape, colour and texture of your beads and found objects. Repeat this process to create three more drops for your wind chime – vary the length of each drop between 23 and 28 cm. When you are making the drops, hold them up together to check that the areas that are going to touch in the breeze will make a noise. Work out the order in which the drops will hang and lay them out on your work surface in that order.

2. Attach your drops to a stick by first attaching one of the central drops. Place the stick between the two pieces of wire and wrap each end tightly around the stick a few times in opposite directions, ending at the bottom of the stick, near the beads. Twist the ends of the wire around each other a couple of times then cut the ends so you have 2 cm long tails (see diagram 4). Feed the tails one at a time back down through the beads to hide them.

3. The distance you place the drops apart will depend on how big your beads and found objects are. The widest objects on the drops need to be about 2 cm apart when the wind chime is hanging still. These drops will be attached to the branch about 5 cm apart from each other.

4. Balance and hang your wind chime by attaching the hanging cord when all four drops are tied in place. Cut a length of jewellery cord about 1 metre long and fold it in half. Pick up your wind chime with two fingers, holding the stick between the two central drops. Slowly move your fingers along the stick until you find the balance point and mark with a pen. Take the second stick and hold it in place at the balance point with the first one.

5. With your other hand pick up the cord at the central point and wrap it twice around both sticks at the balance point. Wind both ends of the cord around the sticks in opposite directions – don't make it too tight just yet. Knot the cord to secure it. Pick up the wind chime by the cord to test it is in the right place; if the wind chime doesn't balance correctly slide the cord along until you find the right position for it.

6. Wrap the two ends of the cord tightly around the sticks in opposite directions, 4 to 5 times. Finish with a tight knot at the top of the sticks. Tie the two ends of the cord securely together to make a loop and hang where it will catch the breeze.

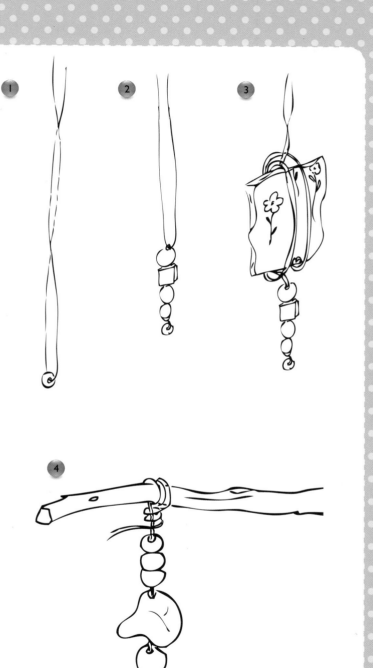

Twinkle Ornament

Ornaments are not just for Christmas time, they are for any time. These twinkly light catchers are perfect to hang at your window or even outside in the garden where they can catch some sun and add some sparkle. These ornaments are made with whatever beads you have on hand, but sparkly ones work best!

project by: kathreen ricketson
suitable for: confident beginners
should take: 1–2 hours

SHOPPING LIST

- Craft wire (22 to 24 gauge)
- Various beads (that will fit onto the craft wire) such as glass and plastic beads, star beads, seed beads and colourful painted beads
- 3 to 4 larger beads with a hole large enough to fit over double twisted wire
- Crimp beads

CRAFTY NEEDS

- Flat-nosed pliers
- Wire cutters

GET READY

- Gather your tools and materials and clear some space on a sturdy worktable. As you are working with beads and other fiddly bits, you will need to work on a clean space. You may need a towel or felt mat to stop your beads rolling everywhere. Make sure you have a comfy chair and some good lighting too.
- You will be using some basic jewellery beads, wire and findings, which can be found at bead or craft shops. You can find a description of basic jewellery techniques on pages 13–14.

HOW TO MAKE THE ORNAMENTS

1. Measure two lengths (20–30 cm) of wire and place a crimp bead over both lengths a third of the way along. Press it into place with your flat-nosed pliers (see diagram 1).

2. String beads along both long ends of the wires, starting with a mixture of 20 small and medium seed beads. Pop in a feature bead, then another 15 seed beads. This should bring you to the halfway mark, where you can place a drop bead or a sequence of pretty larger beads, then continue around with 15 seed beads, a feature bead and 20 more seed beads to finish off. Place some masking tape at the end to prevent the beads slipping off while you string the other wire in the same way, but this time use fewer seed beads at the beginning and end to make it a bit shorter.

3. When you have strung both long ends of wire, place a crimp bead over both ends of the wire, push it up close to the beads and press with pliers to hold in place (see diagram 2). Take the leftover ends of the beaded long wires and bring them up to where you placed the first crimp bead. Twist all four wire tails together with four twists (see diagram 3), then use wire cutters to cut the two shorter tails, leaving the longer tails still pointing upward.

4. Place 2 to 3 mediums beads with a large hole over the two top lengths of wire, and over the twisted wires and wire tails to hide them. Place a couple more beads and place a crimp over both wires again to hold these beads in place.

5. Separate the remaining two lengths of wire at the top, and thread two crimps over one of the wires, then thread the end of the other wire through the crimps to form a loop at the top. Adjust the two crimps so they are around both bits of wire and crimp them into position to hold your top loop in place (see diagram 4).

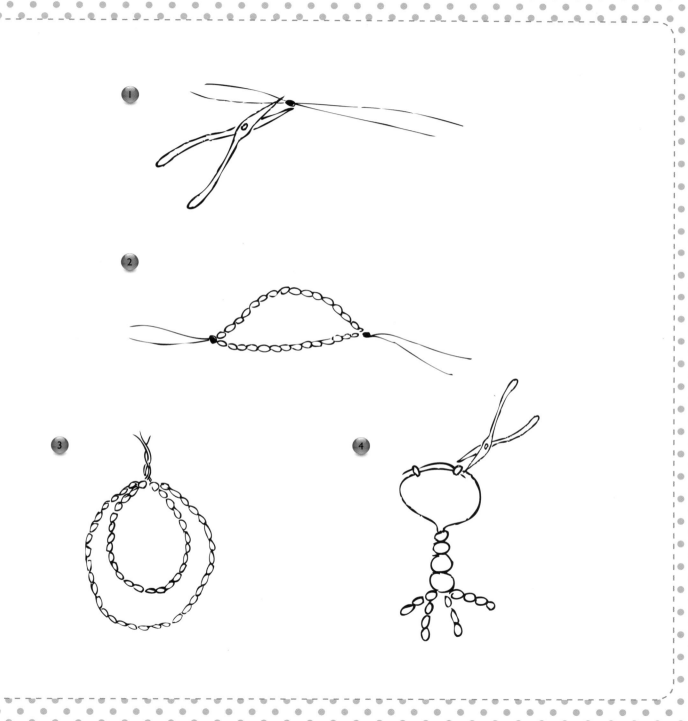

Pentagram Web Sun Catcher

This sun catcher is made with twisted wire and just a couple of beads. It's a pentagram spider web with a beady spider dangling from it. A pentagram is a star with five points; formed by five straight lines, you can draw it without taking your pen off the paper. This star is a little challenging to make, but it will look super cool hanging in your window or in the garden.

project by: rob shugg
suitable for: confident beginners
should take: 2–3 hours

SHOPPING LIST

- 16 gauge enamelled craft wire, 45 cm and 50 cm lengths
- 26 gauge enamelled craft wire, 60 cm and 20 cm lengths
- 5 red medium seed beads
- 5 blue medium seed beads
- 2 medium/large black beads for the spider
- 15 cm of beading string

CRAFTY NEEDS

- Wire cutter
- Pliers
- Tape measure
- Felt-tip pen

GET READY

- Gather your tools and materials and clear some space on a sturdy worktable. As you are working with beads and other fiddly bits, you will need to work on a clean space. You may need a towel or felt mat to stop your beads rolling everywhere. Make sure you have a comfy chair and some good lighting too.
- You will be using some basic jewellery beads, wire and findings, which can be found at bead or craft shops. You can find a description of basic jewellery techniques on pages 13–14. When choosing your beads make sure you can thread your beads easily through the fine 26 gauge wire at least twice and that threading the wire through four times is still possible even if it is a tight fit.

HOW TO MAKE THE PENTAGRAM

1. Take the longer length of the sturdy 16 gauge wire, find the centre and made a 1 cm loop. Make two twists in the wire to hold the loop in place (see diagram 1)..

2. Lay the looped wire out straight alongside the shorter wire. Twist them together as tightly as possible along their entire lengths (see diagram 2). Measure to ensure both halves are the same and cut with the wire cutters if necessary. With your pliers, create loops on each end and join together to form your twisted wire into a circle shape. Mark out five even points around your circle with a felt-tip pen.

3. Take your 60 cm length of fine 26 gauge wire and fold it in half. We will call the right side wire A and the left side wire B. Thread it through the topmost point of your circle, underneath the loop. Slide a red bead onto wire A and thread wire B through the bead, so that the bead holds the wire firmly in place (see diagram 3).

4. Thread two blue beads and one red bead onto both wire A and wire B. With your circle laid flat in front of you, take wire B to the bottom right marked point, loop it around the hoop and back through the red bead. Repeat this process for wire A.

5. Take wire B and add another blue bead (see diagram 4). Thread the wire through the second blue bead on wire A and up toward the top left marked point.

6. Take wire A and thread through the recently added blue bead and on through the second blue bead of wire B toward the right top marked point (see diagram 5). Loop around the hoop and back through the red bead, securing it firmly, then thread through the bead on wire B and then up through the bead on wire A, ending at the top left marked point. Adjust and tighten the wires and bead placement to neaten up your star shape.

7. Wrap both pieces of wire around the hoop and back through the bead to finish the star. You may need to use your pliers to get all four ends of the wire through this final bead. Trim the wire tails with your cutters close to the bead.

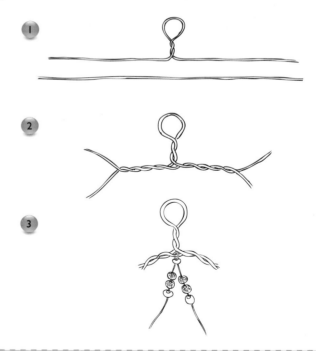

4 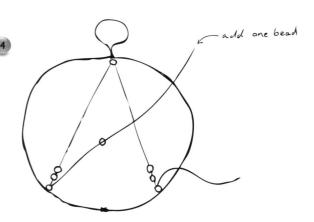 — add one bead

5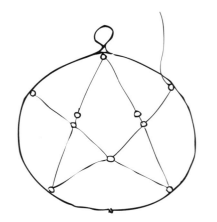

HOW TO MAKE THE SPIDER

1. Take two black beads, one for the spider body and one for the abdomen. Cut four 8 cm long pieces of the fine 26 gauge wire. Fold each piece in half.

2. Take one of the folded wires and thread both beads (see diagram 6) onto it, leaving a small loop at the bottom. Form the front legs with the ends – this wire holds the spider together.

3. Poke the three remaining wires in through either side to come out in between the two beads forming the six centre legs (see diagram 7).

4. Tie a piece of cotton twine onto the tail end of the spider and the bottom of the hoop. Hang your sun catcher star-shaped spider web from a tree outside or hang it in your window to catch the sun.

1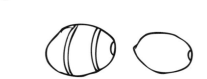

2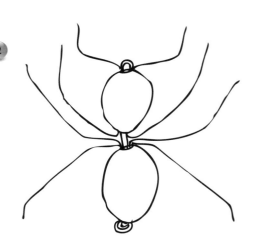

A Seaside Treasury

Take a walk along the beach and you'll find lots of little treasures just begging to be collected. Gather seashells with natural holes and driftwood from the water's edge. Attach them to some string and add some woollen pompoms and felt beads, plus some natural wooden beads, buttons and feathers to make a stunning beach-themed beaded door or window curtain.

project by: cate holst
suitable for: confident beginners
should take: 2–3 hours

SHOPPING LIST

- 20 metres beading cord
- 1 ball of pompom nubbed yarn
- 1 metre long found stick (or a length of dowel) to use as a curtain rod
- Found driftwood sticks
- White paint suitable for wooden surfaces
- Wooden beads and buttons
- Shells with naturally formed holes (or use a drill to form holes)
- Yarn to make 30 pompoms in a mix of green, teal, navy and beige
- White feathers
- White modelling clay
- Curtain brackets or removable hooks

CRAFTY NEEDS

- Paintbrush
- Drill and clamps (optional)
- Pompom maker (optional)
- Rolling pin and butter knife
- Skewer
- Scissors, pencil and ruler
- Long embroidery needle

GET READY

- Gather your tools and materials and clear some space on a sturdy worktable. As you are working with beads and other fiddly bits, you will need to work on a clean space. For working with glue you should wear protective clothing and cover your workspace with newspaper. You may need a towel or felt mat to stop your beads rolling everywhere. Make sure you have a comfy chair and some good lighting too.

Take care when using a hot glue gun, an iron, an oven, a drill or sharp tools. Read the safe handling of craft tools section on page 17 and be sure to put everything away when you are done.

HOW TO PREPARE YOUR BEADS

1. Wash all dirt and sand from your driftwood, sticks and shells. Paint all the wood pieces including the stick or curtain rod with white paint. Drill holes into the shells and driftwood sticks (or knot cord or twist wire instead). Please get parental permission before using a drill. Drill your beads with a piece of reject wood underneath to protect your workbench at all times. Be sure to drill slowly and in control at all times. If you are uncomfortable using a drill, this project can be accomplished without one.

2. Create your pompoms either with a pompom maker or your fingers (see diagrams 1 and 2). You will need about 30 pompoms in several colours.

3. Create modelling clay shell beads by rolling out the modelling clay to 8 mm thick. Insert a wooden skewer down the centre, press shells on either side to create a shell impression and trim your clay with a butter knife around the shell shape (see diagram 3). Ensure the skewer can rotate easily through the material. Bake in the oven using the manufacturer's instructions. Remove from the oven and remove the skewer.

HOW TO PREPARE YOUR CURTAIN ROD

1. Mark your curtain rod into 7 cm intervals with a pencil (13 intervals in total). On the edge of a workbench, clamp the curtain rod. Drill medium sized holes through your marked points (see diagram 4). Or, you can simply knot and glue the cords instead.

2. Attach curtain brackets or removable hooks above your door or window where you will be hanging your beaded curtain.

HOW TO MAKE THE CORDS AND BEADING

1. On a large table or the floor, lay out your curtain rod and cut your cord lengths. Cut seven lengths of beading cord 2.8 metres long. Cut six lengths of pompom nubbed yarn two metres long.

2. Lay out your cord lengths underneath your rod. Begin with a length of beading cord then alternate with the pompom yarn, finishing with the beading cord. Tie these onto your curtain rod. Position the bead elements (shells, pompoms, etc) along the beading cord until you are happy with the composition.

3. Thread a long embroidery needle with the first length of beading cord, and thread the bead elements, spacing them out with knots and ending with a piece of painted driftwood. When attaching the feathers, roll the cord in your fingers to separate the fibres and insert the feather between the fibres. Tie off and glue. Repeat until all beaded cords are threaded.

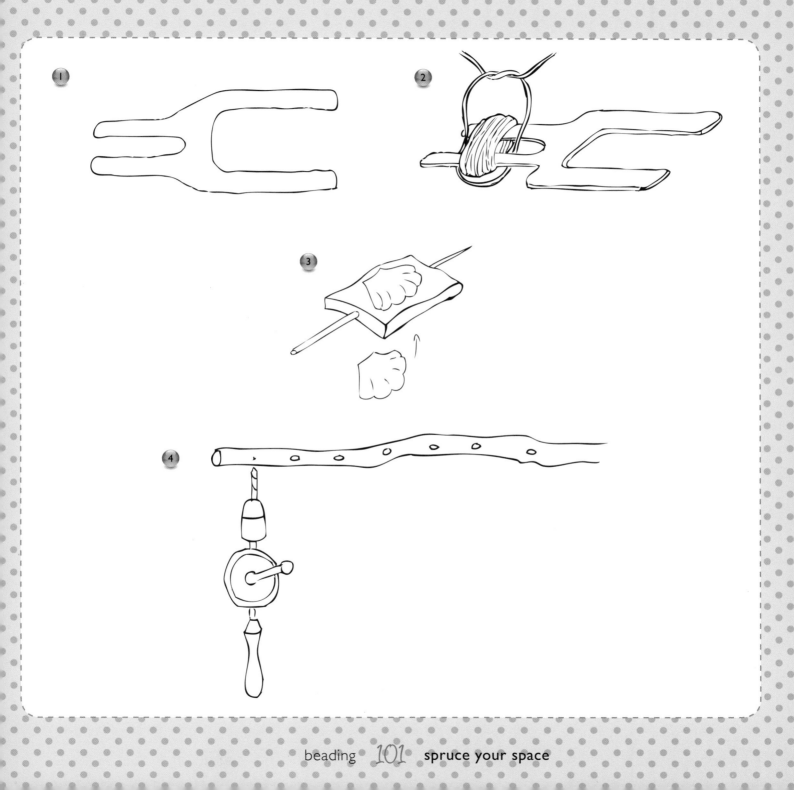

giving is good

Whether it's for a birthday, *Christmas or just because, there is nothing better than making and giving a handmade gift. Friendship pins and bracelets are perfect to make with buddies, beaded cards are very special and all your friends will want a jewel tote. Of course you will want to create some gorgeous goodies for yourself as well. Whatever you like to make and whoever you are making it for, you will find plenty of inspiration here*

The projects in this section range from super easy to a bit trickier. None of them are very difficult, although some designs might take a bit more patience than others. Some projects require a hot glue gun or a needle and thread. If you aren't sure about anything read the techniques section first and ask for help if you need it. Don't fuss about perfection, the aim is to be creative, make something cool and enjoy the process. Get comfy, play your favourite song and make, make, make!

Macramé Bracelet

Paper Bead Ribbons

The Beaded Friendship Pin

Jewel Tote

Woodland Beaded Cards

Button Friendship Band

Macramé Bracelet

Colourful strings, a bunch of beads and a few simple knots are all you need to make these funky bracelets. They're absolutely fun to make and, even better, you can make them in no time! Invite your friends for a macramé beading session; make them as a birthday gift or a best friend's keepsake. But be sure to make plenty, as everyone will love these little goodies!

project by: pascale mestdagh
suitable for: confident beginners
should take: 2–3 hours

SHOPPING LIST

- 2 lengths of waxed cotton cord in different colours, 90 cm each
- Medium sized letter beads with a big opening

CRAFTY NEEDS

- Scissors
- A clipboard, safety pin (or a friend!) to hold the bracelet in place while knotting

GET READY

- Gather your tools and materials and clear some space on a sturdy worktable. As you are working with beads and other fiddly bits, you will need to work on a clean space. Make sure you have a comfy chair and some good lighting too.
- You will be using some basic knots to make this project. Read the basic knotting section on pages 15–16, which explains some techniques. It is a good idea to practise making some square knots before you start making a bracelet.
- For this bracelet, letter beads are slipped onto the two middle strands and are kept in place by knotting around them. Of course other types of beads would work equally well, but keep in mind that, as the beads have to fit over two strands of cord the beads must have a big enough hole. Hemp cord is

often used for macramé. However, you can use any material that allows knotting: embroidery or beading thread, leather, and fabric strips, waxed cotton cord, even scoubidou lace. Depending on the thickness and flexibility of the material used the outcome will be different; thicker cords will result in a wider bracelet and require fewer knots than when using a thinner thread or yarn. Try several materials to obtain different styles, or combine different materials in one bracelet.

HOW TO MAKE THE BRACELET

1. Take two strands of cord in different colours and fold them so that the middle strands are half as long as the two outer strands. For example, if the total length of each of the cords used is 90 cm, fold each one so the middle is 30 cm, and outside is 60 cm (see diagram 1). This is because the knotting uses up cord, making the outer strands shorter every time you add a new knot, while the middle strands won't change in length since they don't do anything (see diagram 2).

2. Lay out the letters in front of you, spacing them out (in between words you need two square knots, in between letters one overhand knot) and make an estimate of how many square knots you need at the beginning and end. Start with a couple of square knots (see diagram 3). Slide the first letter over the two middle strands and push it all the way up.

Tie it into place with a left-handed overhand knot (see diagram 4). Pull the strands to make it firm but avoid pulling too hard so the bead doesn't pop out again.

3. If you're doing a word: slip on the next letter. When doing a phrase: make two square knots before slipping on the next letter. Continue repeating this process until all beads have been tied into place; then finish off with a couple of square knots.

4. Tie the ends, two by two, in a knot, to secure. Use the loose ends to tie the bracelet around your wrist, going through the loop. Cut off the excess ends if necessary.

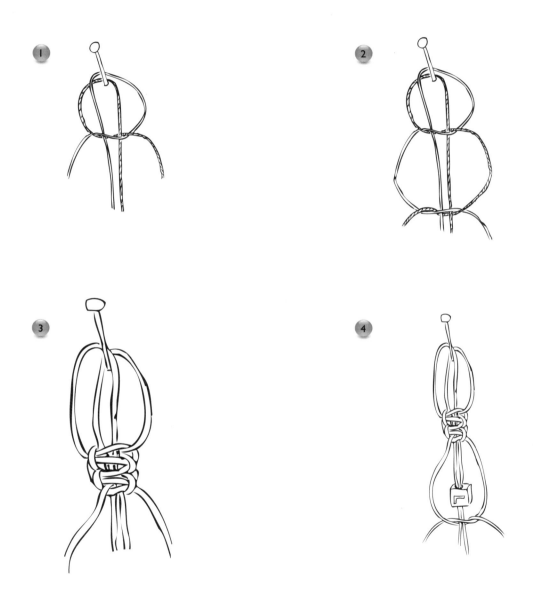

Paper Bead Ribbons

This project will teach you two techniques: how to make paper beads, and how to make a sweet and colourful bookmark with your handmade beads. You will be making this project in two simple stages and will need to leave time for the glue on the beads to dry in between. These would make great gifts for friends or family.

project by: holly keller
suitable for: beginners
should take: less than 1 hour

SHOPPING LIST

- Several sheets of brightly coloured paper (or old magazines, newspapers or wrapping paper)
- 10 brightly coloured beads, 6 mm diameter
- 5 strips of ½ cm wide ribbon in bright colours, each strip 40 cm long
- Glitter
- White wooden bead, 1 cm diameter

CRAFTY NEEDS

- Glue stick or squeeze bottle
- Scissors
- Pencil and ruler
- Small paintbrush or straw

GET READY

- Gather your tools and materials and clear some space on a sturdy worktable. As you are working with beads and other fiddly bits, you will need to work on a clean space. For working with glue you should wear protective clothing and cover your workspace with newspaper. Make sure you have a comfy chair and some good lighting too.

HOW TO MAKE YOUR PAPER BEADS

1. Using your ruler and pencil, mark 2.5 cm wide strips on your paper. Cut these out and cut a pointed end on each strip (see diagram 1). If you want to change your bead shape, just change the shape of your original triangle paper base. The longer your paper triangle strip is, the thicker your bead will be, and the wider the base the longer the bead will be.

2. Use a glue stick or squeeze bottle to run a line of glue from the pointed tip of the paper strip down to about 3 cm from the wider end (don't put glue all the way to the end as this will make it tricky to remove the bead once rolled). See diagram 2.

3. Take your small paintbrush (or straw) and, starting at the wide end, wrap the paper triangle strip around the paintbrush handle, glue-side on the inside. Wrap the paper firmly (but not too tight), and take care to keep the paper centred as you roll so the tip of the triangle ends in the centre of the bead when you finish rolling it (see diagram 3). Slide the bead from the paintbrush handle and coat with more glue. To make sparkly paper beads, roll them in glitter while the glue is still wet, then leave to dry for a few hours or overnight before using.

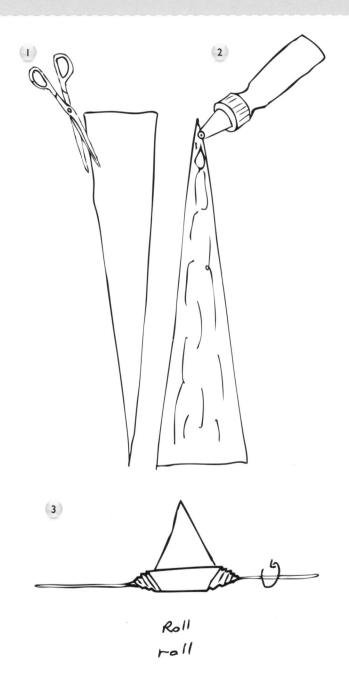

Roll
roll

HOW TO MAKE THE BOOKMARK

1. Take your five lengths of ribbon (40 cm long and all different colours) and place the ends together. Make a loose slipknot about 2.5 cm from one end, and a tighter knot 12 cm from the other end.

2. Working from the longer ribbon end, first separate the ribbon strands and thread each of them with a wooden bead, a paper bead, then another wooden bead and knot the end (see diagram 1).

3. Unknot the other end, slide your white wooden bead into place and re-knot above the bead, using a tight slipknot. Place another slipknot on the other side of the bead in order to hold it into place (just as you did with the beads on the other end).

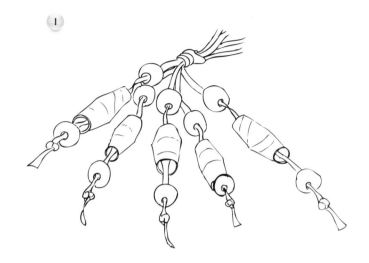

The Beaded Friendship Pin

This is the perfect way to celebrate a good friend's birthday. All you need are a few simple bits and pieces from your local bead shop and some good music in the background to produce this really beautiful pin.

project by: **nanette louchart-fletcher**
suitable for: **beginners**
should take: **less than 1 hour**

SHOPPING LIST

- Assortment of seed beads and other smallish beads in different shapes and sizes
- A large safety pin or a jewellery pin
- Cotton thread
- Scraps of fabric

CRAFTY NEEDS

- Felt mat
- Scissors
- Hot glue gun or cement glue

GET READY

- Gather your tools and materials and clear some space on a sturdy worktable.

As you are working with beads and other fiddly bits, you will need to work on a clean space. For working with glue you should wear protective clothing and cover your workspace with newspaper. You may need a towel or felt mat to stop your beads rolling everywhere. Make sure you have a comfy chair and some good lighting too.

- Take care when using a hot glue gun or jewellery cement glue as they can give off toxic fumes. Be sure to work in a well-ventilated space. Read the safe handling of craft tools section on page 17 and be sure to put everything away when you are done.
- You will be using jewellery findings and small glass beads, which can be found at bead or craft shops. You can find a description of basic jewellery techniques on pages 13–14.

HOW TO MAKE A FRIENDSHIP PIN

1. Neatly lay out all your materials on your felt mat.

2. Cut 8 to 10 lengths of cotton thread, each 15 cm. Knot these tightly over the bar of the safety pin and dab on jewellery glue to secure them in place (see diagram 1). Cut these to slightly different lengths, but leave enough space to knot off the ends after you put the beads on.

3. This is the really fun bit: start threading your beads onto each of the threads. You might want to freestyle it like we've done here or you could create a pattern. Once you finish threading the beads, make sure you firmly knot the ends of the threads and clip any left-over pieces (see diagram 2). Add a dab of glue to the knots to secure them.

4. After threading on all your beads (see diagram 3), further embellish the pin by taking small scraps of fabric and winding them around the top metal bar (see diagram 4). Secure the fabric ends with a dab of glue. All finished! There's just enough time to pack it up in a cute little box for your BFF.

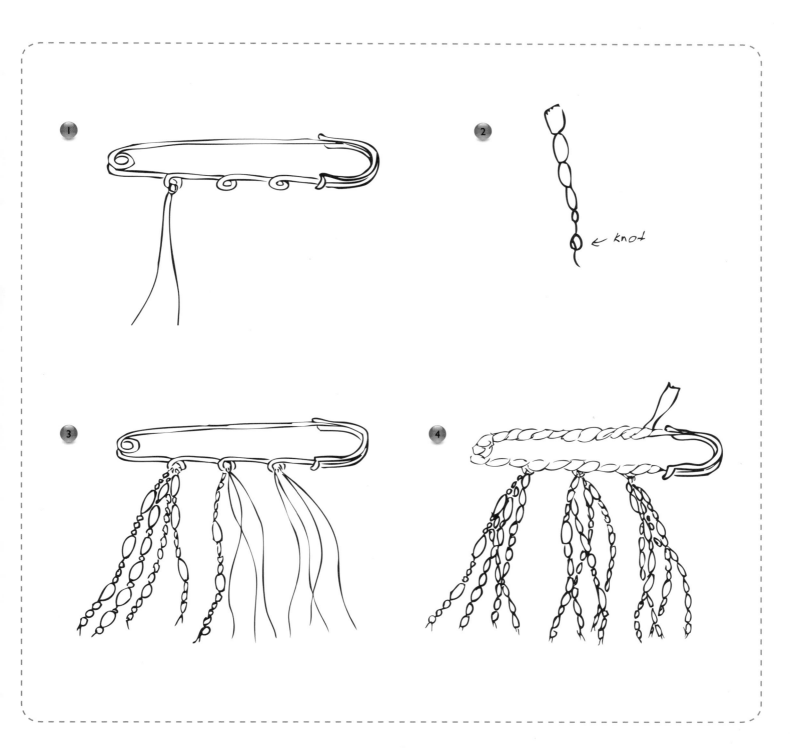

knot

Jewel Tote

This tote bag project will soon bring a little sparkle to your day! It is made from a basic cotton tote bag purchased at a craft store and then embellished with simple plastic jewels and some glue. Try making up your own design and add your own special sparkle to your life.

project by: holly keller
suitable for: beginners
should take: 1–2 hours

SHOPPING LIST

- 1 blank cotton, canvas or hemp tote bag (at least 30 cm square)
- 1 pack of acrylic flat-back jewels
- Sheet of scrap paper

CRAFTY NEEDS

- Masking tape and scissors
- Large embroidery needle
- Black fine-tip marker
- Hot glue gun

TEMPLATES

- There are two jewel tote templates to choose from for this project. Or, you can get really creative and make your own.

GET READY

- Gather your tools and materials and clear some space on a sturdy worktable. As you are working with beads and other fiddly bits, you will need to work on a clean space. For working with glue you should wear protective clothing and cover your workspace with newspaper.
- Take care when using a hot glue gun or jewellery cement glue as they can give off toxic fumes. You must work in a well-ventilated space. Read the safe handling of craft tools section on page 17 and be sure to put everything away when you are done. If you accidentally get some hot glue on the bag, rub it off with a scrap of paper right away. Test the gun on a piece of paper before using it on your tote so you get a sense of how much glue you need to attach one jewel.

HOW TO MAKE A JEWEL TOTE

1. **DIY design:** You can make your own design on the computer in a word-processing program by arranging 1 cm dots to form a design. Also try printing out the first letter of your name in large font on card stock, cut out and trace it onto your bag then glue your jewels as per the instructions here around the edges and on the inside of your letter to make a monogram tote.

2. Photocopy or trace the template, or your own design, onto a sheet of paper. Leave a 2.5 cm border around the design when you cut it out. Place the design in the centre of your tote (or wherever you would like it) and tape down the edges with masking tape (be careful not to cover up any of the design with tape). Warm up your hot glue gun.

3. Insert two sheets of scrap paper inside your tote, just behind your taped-on design, to protect the back of your bag. Take your embroidery needle and poke small holes in the centre of each dot on the design. Take a fine-tip black marker and make a dot onto the tote, through each of the holes on the template (see diagram 1). Remove the template and check your design.

4. Take your jewels and lay them out on your table near you. Following your design, decide on colour and shape placement.

5. Starting in the centre of your design, use your hot glue gun to place a teensy dab of hot glue onto a dot on the fabric. When using the hot glue gun, gently rub the tip of the gun against the fabric before you pull it back to prevent long spider-web-like strings of hot glue. Working quickly, place the flat back of the jewel into the dab of hot glue on the tote. Repeat until you have placed a jewel over every dot in the design (see diagram 2).

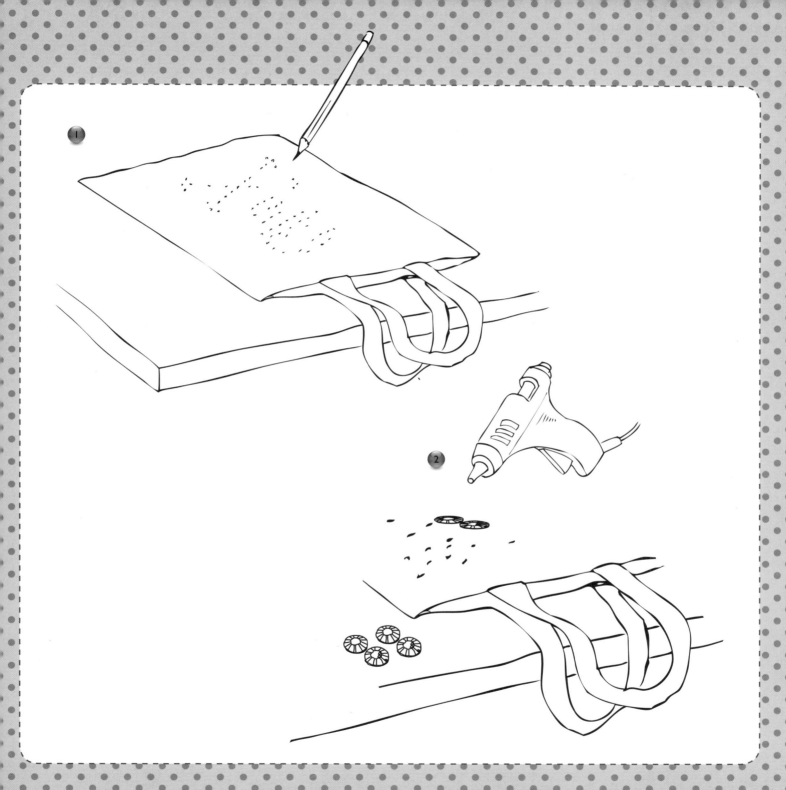

Woodland Beaded Cards

Make a special woodland greeting card for your friends and family next time a birthday comes around. All you need are some bright and sparkly seed beads. Choose from a fox, rabbit or owl, or use the technique described here to design your own card. These cards are so seriously fun to make that you will be handing them out to all your friends.

project by: sharon baldwin
suitable for: confident beginners
should take: 1–2 hours

SHOPPING LIST

- Blank card
- Seed beads in a variety of colours

CRAFTY NEEDS

- PVA craft glue
- Scissors
- Pin
- Paintbrush
- Cotton bud

TEMPLATES

- There are three templates to choose from for this project: fox, rabbit or owl. Or, you can get really creative and make your own.

GET READY

- Gather your tools and materials and clear some space on a sturdy worktable. As you are working with beads and other fiddly bits, you will need to work on a clean space. For working with glue you should wear protective clothing and cover your workspace with newspaper. You may need a towel or felt mat to stop your beads rolling everywhere. Make sure you have a comfy chair and some good lighting too.

HOW TO MAKE

1. Trace or copy the animal template of your choice onto the front of the card (see diagram 1). You could also use a photocopier to enlarge the design to create some wall art if you like.

2. Starting on one side of your design, use your paintbrush to spread craft glue in one section at a time. Cover the glued area with seed beads. Use a pin to pick up and arrange the beads neatly, filling all the little gaps (see diagram 2). Use plenty of glue (it will dry clear and help keep the beads in place) but try not to get any outside the lines. Wait for this area to dry, before repeating this step with the remaining areas.

3. Wipe away excess glue with a cotton bud moistened with water (see diagram 3). Wait until the glue is completely dry before using your card – you might need to let it harden overnight.

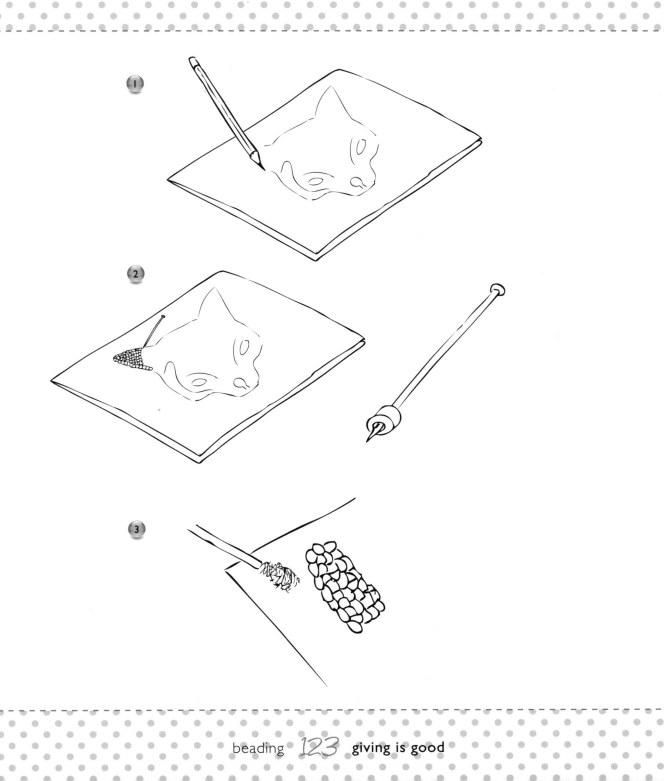

Button Friendship Band

These bracelets are made with a square knot, using four cords. The two middle cords are called filler cords and the outer cords are the knotting cords. Beads and vintage buttons make these square knotted bracelets really special. All you need is some cord, beads and buttons – and a friend to help you – and you are away.

project by: heather elizabeth
    abernathy-graham
suitable for: beginners
should take: 2–3 hours

SHOPPING LIST

• 12 to 14 small beads (or 28 to 32 beads for the wide bracelet)
• 1 medium sized button (or a large button for the wide bracelet)
• 80 cm length of 1 mm hemp cord; plus a 160 cm length of 1 mm hemp cord (or for the wide bracelet four 125 cm lengths of 1 mm hemp cord)

CRAFTY NEEDS

• A clipboard or safety pin to hold the bracelet in place while knotting
• Scissors
• Clear nailpolish or PVA craft glue

GET READY

• Gather your tools and materials and clear some space on a sturdy worktable. As you are working with beads and other fiddly bits, you will need to work on a clean space. For working with glue you should wear protective clothing and cover your workspace with newspaper. You may need a towel or felt mat to stop your beads rolling everywhere. Make sure you have a comfy chair and some good lighting too.
• It is a good idea to practice making some square knots before you start this bracelet. You will also be using various beads and buttons. Make sure your beads and buttons have holes large enough to thread onto the hemp cord. You will use glue or nail polish to keep the cut ends of the cord from fraying.

HOW TO MAKE THE NARROW BRACELET

1. Take your 80 cm length and 160 cm length cord and find the midpoint of both by folding each in half. The two halves of the shorter cord will be the filler cords. The two halves of the longer cord will be the knotting cords. Knot the shorter cord around the midpoint of the larger cord, leaving a loose loop for fastening the bracelet later.

2. Make a series of four square knots (pages 15–16) then thread a bead onto both of the outermost cords. Continue this pattern of knotting and adding beads until you have four sets of square knots. Don't add beads after the last set.

3. Thread the button onto one of the filler cords. If the button has four holes, use each filler cord to go through one set of holes. Continue the pattern of a series of four square knots and two beads. When you have made four series from the button, test the bracelet for size. If it is not yet long enough, add another series of four square knots.

4. Clip the centre filler cords just slightly longer than the finished bracelet and thread the medium sized bead onto one of the knotting cords. Tie both filler cords into a simple knot. Clip off the extra cord and dab some nailpolish or glue onto the cord ends to prevent them from fraying.

HOW TO MAKE THE WIDE BRACELET

1. Cut four cords each 125 cm long. Find the midpoint of all four cords and fold each in half. Make a knot in one cord around the midpoint of the other three cords. Leave a loose loop for fastening the bracelet later (see diagram 1).

2. First make two square knots. Next take the middle four cords and use them to make a single square knot (the two outer cords on each side will remain unknotted). This pattern of knots is called alternating square knots (see diagrams 2 and 3). Thread a small bead onto each of the outermost cords (see diagram 4). Continue with this pattern until you have made eight complete series of alternating square knots. Don't add any small beads after the last series.

3. Thread the button onto one of the two centre cords (see diagram 5) and add another eight series of alternating square knots and beads. Test the bracelet for size and add more series of knots and beads until it is long enough. For the very last series of square knots, skip the middle knot and the small beads.

4. Thread the medium-sized bead onto one of the centre cords. Make a simple knot with the two centre cords to tie on the bead. Clip off the extra cord a few centimetres past the bead and clip off the three outer cords on each side, cutting very close to the knots. Use glue or nailpolish to coat the cut ends of the cord to keep them from fraying.

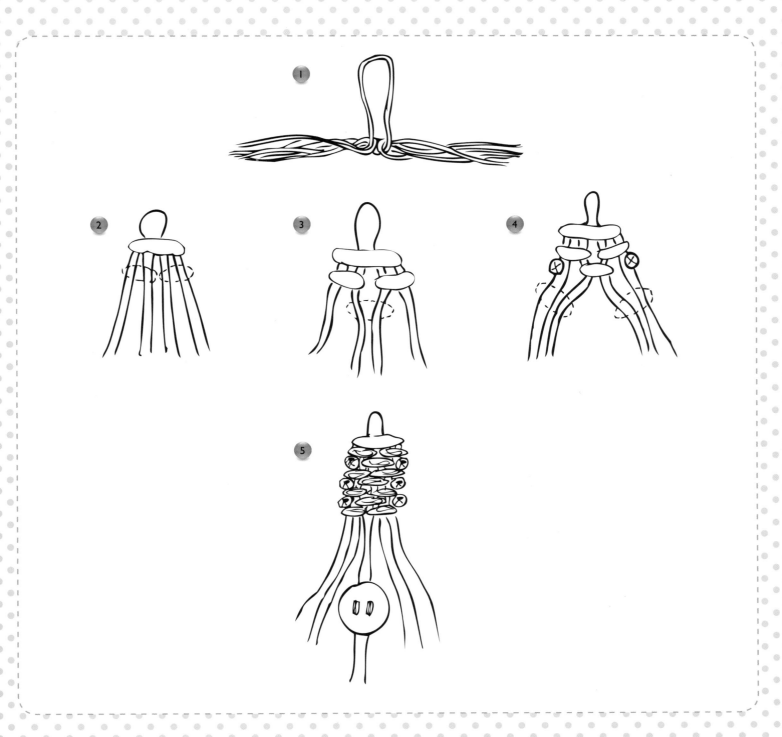

Published in 2011 by Hardie Grant Books

Hardie Grant Books (Australia)
Ground Floor, Building 1
658 Church Street
Richmond, Victoria 3121
www.hardiegrant.com.au

Hardie Grant Books (UK)
Second Floor, North Suite
Dudley House
Southampton Street
London WC2E 7HF
www.hardiegrant.co.uk

National Library of Australia Cataloguing-in-Publication Data is available
ISBN: 9781742700458 (hbk.)

Publisher: Paul McNally
Project editor: Jane Winning
Design and art direction: Heather Menzies
Photography: Alicia Taylor
Styling: Rachel Vigor
Editor: Catherine Etteridge

Colour reproduction by Splitting Image Colour Studio
Printed in China by 1010 Printing International Limited